Ho‌ Illustrations

By

Tony Llewellyn

Published by
Aussie Worship
4 High Street West, Ararat, Victoria, 3377, Australia

HOT SERMON ILLUSTRATIONS
© Tony Llewellyn 2011

ISBN 978-1461168508

About The Author

Tony Llewellyn is an author, Bible teacher, musician and composer. Since coming to Christ in 1975, he has held positions of leadership in most facets of church life, and began pastoring in 1989.

Pastor Tony has a heart to see God's Word loved, understood, and lived out in the lives of Christians everywhere. He believes that when God's people live God's Word they become the fruitful people God wants them to be.

Other Books By Tony Llewellyn

If God Is A God Of Love

Waging War In The Spirit

The Alcohol Question

Successful Songwriting

Spot On Skits (co-written with his wife Alli)

Accelerated Guitar Course

Getting To Know Jesus

Guitarists' Scale Manual

Music Theory For The Contemporary Musician

Understanding The Trinity

How To Mess Up Your Life

Roles and Practical Aspects of Worship Team Members

Modern Piano Technique

Preface

This book is written for those who deal with words. Although the title suggests that it is for preachers, it is equally useful for other public speakers, trainers and writers.

For those of us who believe that we have a teaching gift, putting together a message that will last thirty to forty minutes is not really that difficult. In fact, preachers are professional public speakers, and many of us do this every single week.

The most difficult part, however, is not figuring out the main points, or developing a theme in logical order. That's what the teaching gift does. The greatest challenge is to make sure that what we say is interesting.

Jesus Himself was an expert at this, and employed a technique that every speaker worth his salt should also use. He told stories, and lots of them.

For those who speak regularly on a variety of topics, the greatest task is finding anecdotes that will illustrate your point adequately, spice up your message, and help it to stay in the mind of the listener.

That's what this book is all about. The intention is to provide you with relevant anecdotes, quotes, jokes, and statistics that will help you in preparing your message.

With that in mind, I need to explain some things. First, as the Scripture says, "There is nothing new under the sun." So many stories have been told, and retold, that it is often difficult to find out where they originated. I have now been collecting the contents of this book (and much more!) for over thirty years, and I never thought that I would one day be putting them into a book.

Which means that some of the anecdotes may have originated elsewhere and I can no longer remember the source. Acknowledgements have been made if I have that information; otherwise, the oversight is not intentional. If the details become available, I will correct this in future editions. Naturally, this is only relevant if I am using exact quotations.

Second, as you look at the references, you will notice that there are some rich sources of great stories that you can easily access yourself. These include *Time Magazine*, *Reader's Digest*, books, newspapers, and more. I encourage you to do the same as I have been doing all these years: Start your own collection. It's really not that hard.

Third, although this book is alphabetically categorised throughout (which is why there is no Table of Contents), some of the anecdotes are relevant to more than one topic. As a preacher, I hate having to think of alternative subject headings when looking for sermon illustrations. I've tried to save you the trouble and so some items are listed more than once.

Finally, don't forget that words have power. The spoken word, as well as the written word, can change lives. The sole purpose of the contents of this book is to help you to do that in the most effective way.

Access To God

Imagine trying to make an appointment with the president of the United States of America. You telephone the White House, tell them who you are and that you'd like to make an appointment. The questions come thick and fast: "Who are you? Where are you from? What is the nature of your inquiry? Can anyone else help you? He's very busy." You probably wouldn't get very far. But if the president's son calls him, he'd get a totally different kind of response. Instead of being fobbed off, he'd hear something like, "Oh yes, I'll put you through right away." His kids can ring up and just say, "Hey, dad, I'll be there in five minutes. I'm gonna drop in and see ya." That's the kind of access we have with God.

I'd never been to a cricket match till a few years ago. Then a friend of mine invited me to go. There was no way he was going to sit in the stalls, sweltering in the sun. Instead, we walked through the front gate, through the stalls and up into one of the private boxes. Air-conditioning, closed-circuit TV, drinks, food, tinted glass windows. How did I get access to such sumptuous viewing? Was it because I'd paid the price? No way! It was because my friend had. Without him I wouldn't have gotten past the front gate. But through him, I had access that most others had been denied.

Accountability

One Sunday morning, a cop in a small town was parked at the kerb when he saw a car swerving all over the road. Taking off in hot pursuit, he pulled the driver over, and recognised him as an alcoholic named Frank. The policeman said, "Frank, you're driving all over the place." Frank said, "I'm just trying to get to church, man." Noticing a bottle on the seat next to Frank, the cop asked, "What's that on your seat, Frank?" "It's just water," said Frank. "Give it to me," the cop demanded. He took a whiff. "That's not water," he said. "That's wine." Frank just looked up to heaven and said, "Wow, He did it again."

Achievement

Ben Jonson was one of the most brilliant playwrights ever to come out of England. As a boy, he was so ugly and his clothing so ridiculous that he was tormented even by his own schoolmaster. In an attempt to escape from his anguish, he spent as much time as possible reading. At 18 years of age, he was working as a bricklayer. But by the time he was in his thirties, he was writing for the court of King James I, and in his late forties was awarded an honorary Master of Arts by Oxford University.

Half the people you know are below average.

While driving along a country road, a man noticed a farmer standing in the middle of a large field. The man stopped, walked over to the farmer and asked, "What exactly are you doing?" "I'm trying to win the Nobel Prize," replied the farmer. "How does that work?" asked the man. "Well," said the farmer, "They give the Nobel Prize to people who are outstanding in their field."

It is not necessary to do extraordinary things to get extraordinary results. Warren Buffett

Jon Krakauer finally reached the summit of Mt Everest 10th May, 1996. Several of those who had climbed with him had died on the way. Later he wrote, "I understood on some dim, detached level that [it] was a spectacular sight. I'd been fantasising about this moment, and the release of emotion that would accompany it, for many months. But now that I was finally here, standing on the summit of Mt Everest, I just couldn't summon the energy to care."

Action

Three men were pondering an important question: If you were kidnapped by pirates and left alone on an uninhabited island, but you were allowed one book, what book would you choose? One answered, 'I would choose Shakespeare." The next man, considering himself to be more spiritual said, "No, I would take a Bible." But the third one said, "I wouldn't choose either. I'd take a book that would show me how to build a boat and sail across the ocean. Then I'd be able to read whatever I wanted."

Inaction: A brand-new Plymouth Belvedere was buried in a concrete vault under the courthouse lawn in Tulsa, Oklahoma, 15th June, 1957. Fifty years later, as the city celebrated Oklahoma's 100th year as a state, they opened the vault. Unfortunately, water had seeped into the vault and the Belvedere was nothing but a pile of rust.

Behold the turtle; he makes progress only when he sticks his neck out.

A man wrote to his girlfriend, "Susie, I love you so much. I would climb the highest mountain, cross the driest desert, sail the most tempestuous seas. See you Sunday if it doesn't rain."

A life of faith is built on action; a life of fear is built on the avoidance of action. Wayne Cordeiro

It is not necessary to do extraordinary things to get extraordinary results. Warren Buffett

Advice

A man decided to wallpaper his bedroom, but had no idea how many rolls he'd need. The man next door had recently done the same job with a room of identical size, so he went and asked, "Murphy, how many rolls of paper did you buy for your bedroom?" "Ten," said Murphy, happy to be of assistance. So the man bought his ten rolls of paper and did the job. The walls looked fine, but he had two rolls left over. "Murphy," he said. "I bought ten rolls like you said for the bedroom, but now I've got two left over." "Dat's funny," said Murphy. "So did I!"

Solomon was the wisest man who ever lived. But there's something about him that's always bothered me – for such a wise guy, he was a real dweeb. Why? For a very simple reason. He failed to take his own advice. There's a saying: knowing is nothing, doing is everything. In what did he fail to take his own advice? The pattern for marriage in Proverbs 5:18 (and he wrote this stuff) is one wife, but Solomon had 1000 (1 Kings 11:3). I did some sums on that. In forty years (1 Kings 11:42), he acquired one wife, on average, almost every two weeks! And, just as God had predicted, it was his wives that turned his heart from God.

Aged & Aging

Despite the protests of family and friends that she would be too old to raise a child, a 70-year-old woman sought fertility treatment to give birth to a baby boy. After leaving the hospital, her relatives paid her a visit. "We've come to take a look at your baby," they said. "Not yet," the old woman replied. Assuming the baby must have been asleep they waited an hour or so and asked again, "Can we see the baby now?" "Not yet," replied the pensioner. More time passed. "Come on! Surely we can see him now!" complained the relatives. "No," said the woman. "So when can we see the new baby?" the exasperated relatives exclaimed. "Just as soon as he cries," replied the woman. "Why do we have to wait until he cries?" the relatives asked suspiciously. "Because I've forgotten where I put him," admitted the woman.

One day, an old man was walking down a country road when a frog jumped out in front of him and said, "If you kiss me I'll turn into a beautiful princess." The old man picked up the frog, carefully putting it in his coat pocket. "Hey, didn't you hear me?" the frog screamed. "Kiss me and I'll turn into a gorgeous, available princess!" The old man said, "At my age I'd be just as happy with a talking frog."

A reporter interviewing a 104-year-old woman asked her, "What is the best thing about being 104?" "No peer pressure," she replied.

A man had only just gotten false teeth fitted. That night, he took them out and put them in a glass of water next to his bed. The next morning, he woke up to find his teeth missing and the glass full of 50-cent pieces.

Socrates was writing his best philosophy at 70. Plato was still a student at 50 and did his best teaching after 60. Bacon wrote his greatest works after 60. Phillips Brooks, one of the world's distinguished preachers, was still a major influence at 84. Gladstone was a leader in politics and intellectual circles at 80. Goethe finished his *Faust* at 82. Victor Hugo wrote *Les Miserables* at 62. Jules Verne was writing with imagination at 70. Noah Webster wrote his dictionary at 70.

Jesus said, "And no one puts new wine into old wineskins; or else the new wine will burst the wineskins and be spilled, and the wineskins will be ruined. But new wine must be put into new wineskins, and both are preserved." (Luke 5:37-38) Wine used to go into skins, and when they got old they became brittle. The new wine of the Holy Spirit can't be contained by old structures like the carnal nature or the Mosaic Law. But it's also true that the older we get the less flexible we can be. Unless we keep our hearts soft and supple by listening to the leadings of the Holy Spirit.

My wife's grandfather died at age 94, and up till he was 90 years old, he was the president of the Returned Serviceman's League in Rockhampton, Australia. Every week, he used to visit "the poor old blokes" in the returned soldiers' home. They used to tell him how hard it was, and that no-one understood. And he'd try to encourage them. The funny thing was, though they were Vietnam veterans, he had been an ANZAC, a veteran of both world wars.

Aged Benefits: If ever held hostage you are likely to be released first. No one expects you to run into a burning building. People no longer view you as a hypochondriac. You can eat dinner at 4:00. There's nothing left to learn the hard way. Things you buy now won't wear out. You enjoy hearing about other people's operations. You can party and the neighbours don't even realise it. You no longer think of speed limits as a challenge. Your back goes out more often than you do. Your eyes won't get much worse. Your supply of brain cells is finally down to a manageable size. Your secrets are safe with your friends because they can't remember them either.

The man who views the world at 50 the same as he did at 20 has wasted 30 years of his life. Muhammad Ali

Advancing years have enabled me to discover: That I started out with nothing and still have most of it; now I have my head together but my body is falling apart; I don't remember being absent-minded; if God wanted me to touch my toes, he would have put them on my knees. Jeanette Bowden

Alcohol

In Marble Arch, London, there is an old pub which used to have a gallows next to it. Prisoners were taken to the gallows to be hanged, but on the way, the horse-drawn cart transporting the prisoner was accompanied by an armed guard who would stop the cart outside the pub and ask if the prisoner would like one last drink. If he replied that he would, it was referred to as "one for the road." But if he refused, that prisoner was "on the wagon."

A teacher took a worm and dropped it in a glass of beer. It died. Then she took another worm and dropped it in some orange juice. It swam around and jumped out of the glass and raced out of the classroom at 100 miles per hour. The teacher asked Johnny, "What does that show?" He replied, "If you've got worms you should drink beer."

On TV, in December 2006, they announced that Gold Lotto had now reached $33 million. Asking people what they'd spend it on, one guy said, "$10 million on parties, $10 million on beer, $10 million on gambling, and I'd waste the rest."

Late one evening, a man stumbled home having clearly had too much to drink. At the door, he

13

removed his shoes and carried them in his hands to avoid waking his wife. Tiptoeing up the stairs to their bedroom, he suddenly missed a step, and fell. He landed heavily on his backside, breaking a bottle of vodka in each hip pocket. He was barely able to stifle a yelp, staggered to his feet, and examined his torn and bleeding bottom in a nearby mirror. Finding a packet of band-aids, he tried as best he could to patch himself up before climbing into bed. The next morning, he awoke in enormous pain and saw his wife glaring at him from across the room. "You came home drunk last night," she said bitterly. "Come on, darling!" he objected. "How could you make such an accusation?" "Well," she said, "It could be the broken glass on the stairs. But the most likely reason is all those band-aids plastered over the downstairs mirror."

An American hotel chain advertised for a Chief Beer Officer. The job required that they visit breweries and select the beers for the hotels' bars and restaurants. They received more than 7,000 applicants from thirty countries.

One Sunday morning, a cop in a small town was parked at the kerb when he saw a car swerving all over the road. Taking off in hot pursuit, he pulled the driver over, and recognised him as an alcoholic named Frank. The policeman said, "Frank, you're driving all over the place." Frank said, "I'm just trying to get to church, man." Noticing a bottle on the seat next to Frank, the cop asked, "What's that on your seat, Frank?" "It's just water," said Frank. "Give it to me," the cop demanded. He took a whiff. "That's not water," he said. "That's wine." Frank just looked up to heaven and said, "Wow, He did it again."

Ambition

Ambition is a poor excuse for not being smart enough to be lazy.

Anger

Grumpy Old Men Top Of Heart Risks. Older men with the highest "anger" scores on a personality test face a three-times higher risk of heart disease than their peers. A study, published in the American Heart Association journal *Circulation*, concluded that the higher the level of anger, the higher risk of heart attack or chest pain. The findings mesh with the conclusion of a study last year that episodes of anger were potent triggers of heart attacks. In that study researchers found that during the two hours after an episode of anger, an individual's relative risk of having a heart attack was 2.3 times higher than the risk for someone who had not been angry. Scientists speculate that anger raises the risk of heart attacks by releasing stress hormones into the bloodstream, increasing the heart's oxygen demand and increasing the stickiness of blood platelets.[1]

Have you ever been in a fight with someone and your words were pretty heated and the telephone rings? Suddenly you're as nice as pie! Notice how quickly you can manage your anger! You've got a lot more control over your anger than you think you do.

A woman was complaining to the director of a large American camping program and relating to him the tragic story of her divorce. He asked, "How long ago was your divorce?" "Two years ago," she replied. "And how many people have you talked to about your divorce this week?" "A few," she said. "How many is

---

[1] *The Sunday Mail* 3/11/96

a few?" "Several," she replied. "How many is several?" "Six!" "You know, if I talked to six people a week for two years about my divorce, I would probably feel like you do. I don't think that I would heal either."

Animals

Three reasons dogs don't use computers: 1. They can't stick their heads out of Windows Vista. 2. They have an irresistible urge to attack the screen when they hear, "You've got mail." 3. The saliva-coated mouse is difficult to manoeuvre.

Anointing

David the anointed non-professional looked at Goliath and saw the God of Israel as a giant and Goliath as a dwarf. He said, "Thank God he's so big. My stones can't miss him." Whereas Eliab, the unanointed professional saw Goliath as a giant and himself as a dwarf. Reinhard Bonnke

Anxiety

Public Health Note: The United States Public Health Service once commented: "No bird ever tried to build more nests than its neighbour. No fox ever fretted because he had only one hole in which to hide. No squirrel ever died of anxiety lest he should not lay by enough for two winters instead of one. No dog ever lost any sleep over the fact that he had not enough bones for his declining years."

I only worry on Wednesdays. Any other day I have a worry I write it down and put it in a box. By the time I get to Wednesday I find most of the worries have been taken care of. J. Arthur Rank, one of the world's major movie producers.

Apologies

An apology hotline created by Jesse Jacobs has enabled people to apologise without actually talking to the person they have wronged. They log thirty to fifty calls each week. Jacobs says, "The hotline offers participants a chance to alleviate their guilt and, to some degree, to own up to their misdeeds."

Assumptions

A preacher visited an old lady from his congregation. As he sat on the sofa he noticed a big bowl of peanuts on the coffee table. "Okay if I have a few?" he asked. "No, not at all," said the old lady. They chatted for an hour and when the preacher stood to leave he noticed that instead of eating a few peanuts, he'd emptied most of the bowl. "I'm really sorry for eating all your peanuts, I meant to eat just a few." "Oh, that's okay," replied the old lady. "Ever since I lost my teeth, all I can do is suck the chocolate from them anyway."

One day, Karl Barth, the famous theologian, was on a streetcar in Switzerland. A tourist got in and sat down next to him. As they went along, they started to talk. "Are you new to the city?" Barth inquired. "Yes," the tourist replied. "Is there anything in particular you would like to see while you're here," asked Barth. "Yes," said the tourist. "I'd love to meet the famous theologian Karl Barth. Do you know him?" "Yes," replied Barth, "As a matter of fact I do. I give him a shave every morning." The tourist left the streetcar very pleased that he had met Karl Barth's barber."

Atheism & Atheists

An atheist apparently brought a case against the upcoming Easter and Passover holy days in Florida.

Hiring an attorney for his case against Christians and Jews and the observance of their holy days, he argued that it was unfair that atheists had no recognised days of their own. The case came before a judge. After listening to the impassioned plea of the lawyer, the judge banged his gavel and declared, "This case is dismissed!" Not wishing to go down without a fight, the lawyer immediately jumped to his feet saying, "Your honour, I object. How can you possibly dismiss this case? Christians have Christmas and Easter. Jews have Passover, Yom Kippur and Hanukkah. Yet my client along with all other atheists have no such days." The judge leaned forward. "Oh, but they do," he said. "Unfortunately, your client is seriously misinformed." The lawyer replied, "Your honour, we are not aware of any specially recognised days for atheists." The judge said, "According to my calendar, April 1st is April Fools' Day. Psalm 14:1 states, 'The fool has said in his heart, "There is no God."' Therefore, it is the opinion of this court that, if your client says there is no God, then he is a fool. Therefore, April 1st is his day. Court is adjourned."

An atheist was shipwrecked. Out alone in the middle of the ocean, he looked up to heaven and prayed, "God, I've never bothered you before. Spare me now and I'll never bother you again."

There is not a devil in the universe that is an atheist. Wayne Cordeiro

The Christian God is a being of terrific character – cruel, vindictive, capricious and unjust. Thomas Jefferson

Each morning, a woman walked to her front gate and shouted, "Praise the Lord!" And each time the atheist next door would yell back, "There is no Lord!" One day she prayed, "Lord, I'm hungry. Please send me some food." The following morning, she discovered a big bag of groceries on her front porch. "Praise the Lord," she shouted. Suddenly, her neighbour jumped from behind a bush. "I told you there was no Lord," he said. "I bought those groceries for you." "Praise the Lord!" the woman said. "He not only sent me groceries, He made the devil pay for them."

An atheist was walking in a forest revelling in the fact that he had ruined a great many Christian meetings and generally been a great thorn in God's side when he heard a noise behind him. Looking round, he saw a great bear. He was terrified and ran looking for a tree that he could climb, but the faster he ran, the faster the bear ran. Suddenly, the man fell over a stump just as the bear reached him. In desperation he called out to God to help him. "So you want My help now," God said. "Does this mean that you want to believe and become a Christian?" "No, no," the man replied. "Not me. Make the bear a Christian." And so God answered the atheist's prayer, and just as the bear was about to tear the man to pieces, he stopped. The man heaved a great sigh of relief. Then the bear raised his eyes to heaven and said, "Lord, for the meal I am about to eat I give You thanks".

The God of the Old Testament is arguably the most unpleasant character in all fiction: jealous and proud of it; a petty, unjust, unforgiving control-freak; a vindictive, bloodthirsty ethnic cleanser; a misogynistic, homophobic, racist, infanticidal, genocidal, filicidal, pestilential, megalomaniacal, sadomasochistic, capriciously malevolent bully.[2]

---

[2] Dawkins, Richard *The God Delusion* p31

Each morning, a woman walked to her front gate and shouted, "Praise the Lord!" And each time the atheist next door would yell back, "There is no Lord!" One day she prayed, "Lord, I'm hungry. Please send me some food." The following morning, she discovered a big bag of groceries on her front porch. "Praise the Lord," she shouted. Suddenly, her neighbour jumped from behind a bush. "I told you there was no Lord," he said. "I bought those groceries for you." "Praise the Lord!" the woman said. "He not only sent me groceries, He made the devil pay for them."

Christianity is the most perverted system that ever shone on man. Thomas Jefferson

Atheism is a non-prophet organisation.

Dial-A-Prayer for atheists: They call the number, it rings, but nobody answers.

Atonement

A judge had to sentence a friend of his for breaking the law. This presented a bit of a dilemma. If he let him off, he would be a good friend but not a good judge. If he sentenced him, he would be a good judge, but not a good friend. He sentenced his friend to pay a fine of $10,000, stepped around the bench and paid his friend's fine.

Attitude

Back in 1979, speaker and author Dennis Waitley once found himself racing to catch a flight. He was on his way from Chicago to Los Angeles and had to board DC10 flight 191 to deliver a speech later in the day. But this time he didn't get there on time. Furious to see the gate agent lock the door just as he arrived, he pleaded with her to open the gate and let him board. She refused, and fuming, Waitley left the boarding area to complain, but only twenty minutes later, the news came through that the plane he had missed had just crashed on take-off, killing everyone on board. Instantly, his anger and disappointment turned to shock, and later to gratitude. He left the ticket line and checked into a room at an airport hotel. He knelt beside his bed and then tried to get some sleep. Instead of returning the unused ticket for a refund, he decided to keep it and put it on his office notice board at home. It's a silent reminder, because every so often if he gets annoyed at something, his wife Susan leads him by the hand through to the notice board to take a look at his flight 191 ticket. Waitley says, "Every day is a gift to be lived to the full."

A father had two sons. One was a pessimist and the other an optimist. He decided he'd really try them out to see how entrenched their natures were. So he filled the pessimist's room with toys and filled the optimist's room with horse manure. He went into the pessimist's room to find him sitting dejectedly on the floor. "What's wrong?" he asked. "Look at all these toys," said the boy. "Someone's going to have to put them all together and read the manuals. Then all the kids in the neighbourhood will want to come over." Then he went to see the optimist, and found him having a ball digging in the manure. "What are you doing?" he asked. "Well, I figure that with all this manure, there's got to be a pony in here somewhere."

Once upon a time a woman woke up one morning, looked in the mirror, and saw that she had only three hairs on her head. "Well," she said, "I think that today I might braid my hair." And she did, and she had a great day. The next morning she woke up, checked herself in the mirror and discovered that she only had two hairs on her head. "Hmm," she said, "Maybe I'll part my hair down the middle today." So she did, and she had a fantastic day. The next morning she woke up, looked in the mirror and found that she had only one hair left on her head. "Well," she said, "Not to worry. Today I'll wear my hair in a pony tail." So she did, and she had the best day. The next day she woke up, looked in the mirror and noticed that there wasn't one single hair on her head. "Hooray!" she exclaimed. "I don't have to do my hair today!"

Two frogs fell into a can of cream,
Or so I've heard it told;
The sides of the can were shiny and steep,
The cream was deep and cold.
"O, what's the use?" croaked No. 1,
"'Tis fate; no help's around.
Goodbye, my friends! Goodbye, sad world!"
And weeping still, he drowned.
But No. 2, of sterner stuff,
Dog-paddled in surprise,
The while he wiped his creamy face
And dried his creamy eyes.
"I'll swim awhile, at least," he said –
Or so I've heard he said;
"It really wouldn't help the world
If one more frog were dead."
An hour or two he kicked and swam,
Not once he stopped to mutter,
But kicked and kicked and swam and kicked,
Then hopped out, via butter!   T.C. Hamlet

In Los Angeles, the Bank of America branch is part of a multilevel building which includes car parks on the lower floors. The bank's customers did not need to pay for parking if they performed a transaction at the bank and had the teller validate their ticket. However, this privilege was eventually withdrawn as customers learned how to take advantage of the system. One day, an old man waited in a long line to have his ticket validated. Finally, when he got the next available teller, he deposited a small amount and asked for his ticket to be validated. The teller obliged and told him there was a small parking fee. "Why?" asked the old man. "You've never charged me before." Seeing the crowd of waiting customers, the teller snapped, "Mister, I don't make the rules. I just have to enforce them." "But I've been with this bank for a long time," the old man replied. "Can't you just validate the ticket like you always have?" "Look," said the teller. "If you don't like it, talk to the manager. I've got a lot of customers waiting." The old man returned to the end of the line. When he again got to the front of the queue, he withdrew $4.2 million, walked across the road and put his money in another bank.

Authority

The enemy can have power without authority. For instance, the Taliban had no authority, but they had power. Cf. Luke 10:18-20

Policemen in India are being offered a monthly bonus of $1 each if they grow a moustache. Authorities say that hair adds to the overall authority of officers.[3]

A man was speeding down the road, doing 90 in a 60 zone. When the police pulled him over, the polite officer said, "Would you mind showing me your licence, sir?" The man replied, "Yup." "Excuse me?" said the policeman. The motorist was feeling pretty tough, so he answered, "I said, 'yup'." The policeman flashed his badge, and repeated, "Your licence

---

[3] *Sunday Mail*, 25th January, 2004

please, sir." The driver blew him a raspberry. "Okay, out of the car pal," demanded the officer. "I don't think so," the man said stubbornly. "I like it here." Suddenly, the policeman drew his gun. He stuck it straight up the man's right nostril, dragged him out of the car, cuffed him, threw him into the squad car, and drove him off to the watch house. When the cop showed his badge, that was a demonstration of authority. When he stuck his revolver in the man's nose and carted him off to jail, he was demonstrating power – the ability to back up that authority. The words that God speaks not only have authority, they have power too.

An old lady returned home from a church service to find an intruder in the process of ransacking her house. "Stop!" she yelled. "Acts 2:38!" (which says, "Repent!") The burglar stopped dead while the old lady called the police. As he handcuffed the burglar, the officer asked, "How come you just stood there? All the old lady did was quote a Bible verse." "A Bible verse?" the thief replied. "She said she had an axe and two .38s!"

Bible (See also God's Word or Scripture)

Men do not reject the Bible because it contradicts itself but because it contradicts them.

It's one thing to say, "I believe the Bible from cover to cover." It's another thing to *know* what's between the covers. Charles Simpson

Sin will keep you from this book. This book will keep you from sin. D.L. Moody

A little boy asked his friend, "Why does your grandmother study the Bible so much?" "I'm not sure," he replied. "I think she's studying for her finals."

Blaming

Ever since the Garden of Eden, it's been human nature to look around for someone to blame. After they had sinned, Adam and Eve heard God walking in cool of day and hid. God asked them a question: "Where are you?" Of course, He already knew where they were. What can God not see? But what happened then has stayed with human nature ever since. Adam blamed Eve, Eve blamed the serpent, and the serpent didn't have a leg to stand on.

Strange isn't it, that if you catch a child hitting her baby sister, her response will almost certainly be something like, "But she hit me first."

Blessing

May peace break into your house and may thieves come to steal your debts. May the pockets of your jeans become a magnet of $200 bills. May love stick to your face like Vaseline and may laughter assault your lips! May your clothes smell of success like smoking tyres and may happiness slap you across the face and may your tears be that of joy. May the problems you had forget your home address.[4]

For those of us who were born in cold countries like Wales, we know what it's like to be cold. It's snowing outside, and it's freezing in bed. And all you want to do is spend your life in front of the fireplace. Imagine what it's like then, when you go to the kitchen sink to get a drink of water, turn on the tap and nothing comes out. There's plenty of water; after all, all it does is rain. And there's nothing wrong with the

---

[4] An email I received.

water supply, or the pipes. But there is a blockage in the pipes. The water has frozen. Sin blocks God's blessing, but obedience to God releases His blessing.

When God opens the windows of heaven to bless us, the devil will open the door of hell to blast us. God's smile means the devil's frown.

Boldness

A great deal more failure is the result of an excess of caution than of bold experimentation with new ideas. The frontiers of the Kingdom of God were never advanced by men and women of caution. J. Oswald Sanders

Think about what happened with the disciples. They were a bunch of chicken-hearts. They all deserted Jesus in His hour of need. Then they got filled with the Holy Spirit and suddenly they're as bold as a lion. That's what the Holy Spirit does.

Business

The owner of a very successful nationwide business asked his new son-in-law to meet with him for lunch. They were enjoying a cup of coffee when the businessman said, "I just wanted to take this opportunity to welcome you into the family. I want the best for you and my daughter, and to give you the best possible financial start, I've made you an equal partner in my firm. "That's great," said the son-in-law. "So, starting next week," continued the businessman, "I'd like you to take charge of factory operations." "But I hate factories," said the young man. "They're too noisy." "Okay," said the businessman. "How about management? You can take control of all our office staff." "I hate offices too," said the son-in-law. "Then I'm not quite sure what you want me to do. I've just made you half-owner of one of the biggest firms in the country. If you won't work in the factory or the office, what do you want?" "I want you to buy me out," said the young man.

Every business is built on friendship. J.C. Penney

Calling

A man asked his pastor, "If Jesus knew Judas was going to betray Him, why did He call him in the first place?" The pastor answered, "I don't know, but here's a harder question: Why did He call me?"

Gina (not her real name) had a call to go to the mission field. She had it all worked out. She'd train as a nurse and that would put her in a prime position to be able to get into a lot of countries. Then along came Simon (not his real name, either). She fell in love and they got engaged. Only problem was that Simon was very clear that he felt no call to go to the mission field. Not long afterwards, a man came to their church to minister. As he was praying for her, God gave him a word: "You are called to the mission field. God wants you to know that the person whom you are planning to marry will lead you away from that calling." What to do? Choose a good thing and marry her sweetheart. Or break it off so that she could attain to God's best? I'm sorry to say she married him. Sometimes the choice isn't between good and evil, it's between good and best. But the prophecy was true. Not only did she turn away from her calling, she also subsequently turned away from the Lord.

The difference between your ability and your calling is the grace of God. Mark Driscoll

Careers

Technicians change 700 light bulbs a week throughout the Sydney Opera House.[5]

Management Terms: Delegate – pass the buck; Pending – I don't know what to do with this; Delayed – forgotten; Frank and open discussion – blazing row; Analytical projection – guess; Forecast – guess again; Ambitious – ruthless; Shrewd – devious; Deficit – staggering loss; Industrial by-product – our waste; Environmental pollution – other people's waste; Pilfering – theft by an employee; Fringe benefit – theft by the executive.

Caring

Why put a live chick under a dead hen? Derek Prince, commenting on the proper nurture of new Christians and the church they go to.

Change

A minister wanted to move a piano that was on the church's stage. There was a disagreement, but the minister insisted and was fired. Five years later, he visited the church and noticed that the piano had been moved. He went to the new pastor and asked, "How did you do that?" "One inch at a time," replied the pastor.

A New Zealander went into a fish and chip shop and said, "$5 worth of fush and chups please." "You're a Kiwi, mate," said the Australian. "Yeah, how'd you know?" "It's the accent, mate. Gives you away every time." The New Zealander went home and practised saying, "Fish and chips." A month later he went back to the fish and chip shop and said, "$5 worth of fush

---

[5] *Readers Digest*, July, 2007 p 23

and chups please." Again, the Australian said, "You're a Kiwi, mate." "Yeah, how'd you know?" "It's the accent, mate. Gives you away every time." The New Zealander went home and practised again. He even got lessons. A month later he went back to the fish and chip shop and said, "$5 worth of fish and chips please." "You're a Kiwi, mate," said the Australian. "Yeah, how'd you know?" "The fish and chip shop closed three weeks ago. This is a stationery store."

A lady sat in my seat in church the other day. She's a very nice person. In fact, she's a good friend and I can sit somewhere else. No big deal. But I like my seat. It's on the right just as you enter the church sanctuary. It's nice because I can rest my arm on the end. It's a good seat, but I wouldn't make a fuss over something as unimportant as a seat, and I never hold a grudge. Actually, you know, it was three months ago she took it and I still don't know why. I've never done anything to her, never taken her seat or anything else. And now I'll have to come to church an hour early just to get my seat. You know, I think she took it deliberately, because it's one of the best seats in the house. And she had no business taking it. I don't see why I should have to go to church two hours early to get what's rightfully mine! That's the way great social injustices begin: inconsiderate people taking other people's seats! It's how revolution start. A person can only take so much, you know. Where will it all end? If someone doesn't do something about it, nobody's seat will be safe. People will sit wherever they want, and next they'll take my parking place, then my home. World order will be in a shambles! Civilisation will come to an end. But hey, I don't really mind.

Farmer Brown and his family had lived out west all their lives, but they had to go to the big city to view some documents. So they loaded up the utility truck and headed to the city. They pulled up outside a massive building and the farmer said to his family, "Stay here. I won't be long." Little Johnny said, "Aw, Dad, can't I come too?" "All right," said the farmer. "But the rest of you stay in the ute." Father and son got out of the truck, and up the steps to the front entrance, when the doors suddenly opened. "Wow, did you see that Dad?" asked the little boy. "The doors just opened by themselves." "Yeah, ya never know what they've got in the city, son." So they wandered around, marvelling at all the things in the building. The farmer asked for directions and the clerk pointed at the lift door. They'd never even seen an elevator before, so they went and stood in front of it, not quite knowing what to make of it. Next thing an old woman came along, got in the lift, and the door shut. A couple of minutes later, the door opened again, and out stepped a beautiful young woman. An old woman went in, and a beautiful young woman came out. The farmer turned to his son, "Quick son, go get your mother." There's a theological truth in this: God isn't interested so much in changing us, as He is in exchanging us at the cross.

An impatient father made an appointment with the university chancellor. He asked if it was possible for his son to complete his three-year degree in less time. The chancellor replied, "Well now, that all depends on what you want your son to be. If you want to grow an oak tree, it will take a number of years. But if all you want is beans, we can do that in just a few months."

God once said to a preacher, "You and I are incompatible, and I do not change."

30

In matters of principle, stand like a rock. In matters of taste, swim with the current. Thomas Jefferson

Character

With great abilities, there is the need for great character. Music is a perfect example. All these people suffered because, although they had great talents, they did not have great character: Jimi Hendrix, Janis Joplin, Kurt Cobain, Keith Moon, Michael Hutchence, Elvis Presley, Liberace, Peter Allen, Tchaikovsky.

Children

A Swedish government study on delinquency in teenagers found that, where parents had conflicting values or were inconsistent in putting their values into practice and tried to hold their children to values they themselves did not live by, their children were not able to internalise their values. In other words, expected by their parents to be more disciplined than the examples set, most of the children turned out to be much less so. What made the difference was how closely the parents lived by the values they tried to teach their children.

The Sunday School teacher was leaving and all the children brought her presents. The florist's daughter brought her a big bunch of flowers. The baker's son brought her a beautiful cake. Then the son of the owner of the local pub handed her a big box. She noticed that something was leaking. Not wanting to appear ignorant of such things, she tasted one of the drops. "Is this a case of white wine?" "No." She tasted another drop. "Is it a case of champagne?" "No." She tried another drop. "Is it brandy?" "No miss, it's a puppy."

A man related the story of how he watched a horse being broken in. It was in a small wooden enclosure and two or three people were pulling on the ropes tied round the horse's neck as the horse kicked frantically. Seeing the horse's bleeding legs the man walked over to the owner and asked, "Must you continue?" The owner replied softly, "Yes, if I don't win this one, no one will ever ride him." You must win round one with your children if you want them to respect your authority.

Footsteps
There are little feet that follow
In my footsteps every day.
Their little voices echo
So much of what I say.
Sometimes I'm not too happy
With all the things I see.
Then I begin to realise
That they're imitating me.
My patience seems to falter
And I speak with too much haste –
Till I hear the Saviour speaking
When I look into each face.
Oh God, please grant me wisdom
As I train each little one,
Help me set a good example
As You Yourself have done.
I would not ask for riches
Or that they famous be,
But may each find Christ as Saviour
And live each step for Thee. Author unknown.

When it's hungry, a baby doesn't think, "I'll wait till later till I cry for food. They've got visitors."

A proliferation of connections between billions of neurons occurs in all children, of course. A child's brain, unlike a computer, does not come into the world with its circuitry hard-wired. It must set up its circuits in response to a sequence of experiences and then solder them together through repeated neurological activity.[6]

A boy said, "Hey Dad, can I use the car?" "Sure, son," said the father. "Just bring your grades up, study your Bible, and cut your hair. Then you can use the car." "But Samson, Moses and Jesus had long hair," argued the son. "Yes, and everywhere they went they walked," replied the father.

A 65-year-old Chilean woman, by the name of Leonita Albina, has had 55 documented births. In total, she claims to have had 64 children.

A teacher was instructing her class of Grade 2 students on personal hygiene. She asked, "Who knows what head lice are?" A little boy put his hand up and answered, "It's what they put on the front of cars."

A ten-year-old boy decided to give his mother a birthday present. He had a $10 note, tied it to his guinea pig, and said to her excitedly, "The guinea pig's got something for you." Then he explained to her that he had intended to give her $5, but thought that wasn't enough. So he decided to give her $7. That's right, he wanted $3 change!

The age of electronic communication has taken on spiritual significance. A young child was heard saying the Lord's Prayer: "And lead us not into temptation, but deliver us some email."

A primary school teacher fell pregnant. A few months later, the bump became obvious and one of her pupils

---

[6] J. Madeleine Nash, *Time Magazine*, 6th May, 2002, p58

said, "Miss, you're getting fat!" The teacher explained that she wasn't actually fat, but that a baby was growing inside her tummy. "Oh!" said the little girl, "But what's growing in your bottom?"

According to one child, angels drink milk from holy cows.

A little boy wrote to his aunt and said, "I'm very sorry that I forgot your birthday. It wasn't very thoughtful and I wouldn't blame you if you forgot my birthday on Friday."

A little girl approached her father while he was watching TV. "Daddy, what's sex?" she asked. Knowing how important it was to answer her questions openly and honestly, he talked about the differences between boys and girls, about how the body changes as children grow up, and how babies were created. She listened attentively, and asked, "And what's a couple?" Her father explained about dating, finding someone special and marriage. Then at the end of his discourse, he said, "So what's brought on these questions?" The little girl replied, "Because I just asked Mummy how long till dinner and she said, 'Just a couple of secs.'"

Choices

When you choose the behaviour, you choose the consequences. Dr Phil McGraw

Chosen

When I was a boy, I used to love playing soccer. Boys lined up so that the captain of each team could choose their players. In particular, I remember the feeling of relief at being chosen and the feeling of pride if I was the first, or one of the first, to be chosen for the team. But then it got to the last one or two.

Usually, those boys weren't liked as much as the others, or weren't as good at sport. So the two captains would argue about who would take the last boys because neither of them wanted them on their team. It was difficult not to feel sorry for them because you know yourself that it doesn't ever feel good not to be wanted. Isn't it good to know God wants you on His team? That before the foundation of the world, God looked through time, and He saw you, and He saw me, and He said, "I'll take him. I'll take her." He didn't leave you till last. He chose you before you even lined up. What a relief to know that you and I didn't get in by accident. That when we came to the Lord to give our hearts to Him, God didn't say, "Let's see, he's repented, he's believing, confessing Jesus as Lord. Aw, darn it, he's fulfilled all the conditions. Now I'll have to honour My word, now I'll have to accept him. And him of all people. He's the last one I would have chosen. How do I get myself into these predicaments?" No, God chose you. You've been selected, part of the team.

Christian

Just because a mouse is born in a biscuit tin, doesn't make it a biscuit. And just because you were brought up in the church, doesn't make you a Christian.

Christmas

Christmas letters from children to Santa: "Dear Santa, you did not bring me anything good last year. You did not bring me anything good the year before that. This is your last chance. Signed, Alfred." Another said: "Dear Santa, there are three little boys who live at our house. There is Jeffrey; he is two. There is David; he is four. And there is Norman; he is seven. Jeffrey is good some of the time. David is good some of the time. But Norman is good all of the time. I am Norman."

Why is Christmas just like any normal day at the office? Because you do all the work and the fat bloke in the fancy suit gets all the credit.

If the three wise men had been three wise women, they would have asked for directions, arrived on time, helped deliver the Baby, cleaned the stable, and made a casserole.

Church – The Body, Its Mission, and Growth

A woman was getting ready for church when her son said, "I'm not feeling well." "You just don't want to go to church," said the woman. "Now get ready as quickly as possible." Part way through the service, she noticed that he was groaning. "What's wrong?" she asked. "I think I'm going to throw up," he replied. "Well, don't do it here. Go outside." The boy stood up and ran for the back door. He was back within a few seconds. "So you didn't throw up, after all?" "Oh yes, but I didn't have to go outside. When I got to the back, there was a box there with a label on it saying, 'For The Sick.'"

Many members can accomplish collectively what the same numbers cannot do individually; an aeroplane is a machine that consists of 100% non-flying parts.

Why put a live chick under a dead hen? (Derek Prince, on proper nurture of new Christians and the church they go to.)

How do you eat a banana? First, you separate it from the rest of the bunch. And that's how the devil destroys Christians too.

Hands are wonderful things. They can type, play the piano, break a piece of wood, or caress someone's hair. But imagine a hand that wants to be a foot. This wonderful work of engineering and design would have to perform a totally different function. You would have to spend all your time walking on your hands. Or imagine a foot that wants to be a hand. Could it ever hope to play the violin? Each member of the body is uniquely designed by God for its particular function.

Can you imagine the heart sulking and saying, "It's not fair. I want to be the eyes. They get to do two things – see things and help determine distances. All I get to do is pump blood. Sometimes I just feel like a useless workhorse."

An Australian biologist has exploded the myth that bees are a hive of order, finding them to be scheming and factional. Dr Ben Oldroyd, a senior lecturer at Sydney University's School of Biological Sciences, says a genetic mutation can make usually sterile female worker bees rebel and lay counterfeit queen bee eggs, causing chaos and destruction in the colony. Normally, only the queen is allowed to lay eggs. If a worker produces any, they are quickly eaten by "police" workers. But in anarchist colonies, rebelling workers lay eggs that are indistinguishable from the queen's. Her power is lessened, workers stop working and the colony – "a scheming mass of conflict with factions trying to outdo each other" – rapidly disintegrates.[7] This is a great lesson for the church.

The eyes see the food; the hands pick it up; the mouth chews it; the swallowing mechanism swallows it; the stomach digests. Any failure by any of these

---

[7] *Reader's Digest* June 2004 p 139. Original source: *Sydney Morning Herald*

parts and you have problems. God is counting on every member of the body of Christ to do their job.

A man was marooned on an uninhabited island. Twenty-five years later, he was rescued, but the rescuer noticed that there were three huts on the island. "What's that one for?" he asked. "That's where I live," said the rescued man. "And what's that one for?" asked the rescuer. "That's where I go to church." "So what's the third one for?" he asked. "That's where I used to go to church," came the reply.

Robert Louis Stevenson wrote in his diary, "I have been to church today, and am not depressed."

The church is a body. No part of my body is part-time.

You've got to admire someone like Nick Vujicic. No arms, no legs. How does he get by? So many of the things that people with normal bodies do and take for granted, he still manages to do. How? Because other parts of his body step up to the mark and do something they weren't necessarily designed to do. For instance, he's got a foot with two toes. And he types with it. Is the foot designed to do things like typing? Of course not. Nobody who has hands would use their toes to type. Nobody who has hands would use their mouth to paint. But there are times when people have to make do with what they've got, and other parts of the body step in and perform a function they weren't originally designed to do. That's often what happens in smaller churches.

It's this principle [living to make others successful] that makes possible the efficient operation of the human body. My lungs cheer for a healthy heart. Why? Not for the heart's sake alone, but also for the lungs' sake. If the heart goes down, so do the lungs.

My stomach cheers on my kidneys. It wants the liver to remain in top form, not only for the kidney's benefit, but also for its own.[8]

Back in 1925, an evolutionist stated at the Tennessee Scopes Trial, that there were no less than 180 vestigial structures in the human body. They believed that all of those structures no longer served a useful purpose, but were leftovers of the evolutionary process. Today we know better. That list has shrunk to almost zero. Even the mysterious appendix is now known to help produce antibodies and prevent bacteria in the colon reaching the blood stream. No body part is useless.

Church Growth

The church that doesn't want to grow is telling the world: We are having such a good time over here, the rest of you can go to hell. Kong Hee

If you're expecting your church to grow by people having their steering wheel turned supernaturally, you're going to have a very small church. Peter Youngren

Anytime someone says, "You can't measure success by numbers," my response is, "It all depends on what you're counting!" If you're counting marriages saved, lives transformed, broken people healed, unbelievers becoming worshippers of Jesus, and members being mobilised for ministry and missions, numbers are extremely important. They have eternal significance.[9]

For those who say that numbers aren't important, imagine this: A couple goes to the beach with their three children. During the course of the day, all of

---

[8] Cordeiro, Wayne *Doing Church as a Team* p218
[9] Warren, Rick *The Purpose Driven Church* p52-53

their children go missing. They search everywhere and finally find two of them. The husband turns to his wife and says, "Let's go. Numbers aren't important."

A great deal more failure is the result of an excess of caution than of bold experimentation with new ideas. The frontiers of the Kingdom of God were never advanced by men and women of caution. J. Oswald Sanders

New construction is always easier than renovation.[10]

Citizenship

Before the colonialists imposed national boundaries on Southeast Asia, the kings of Laos and Vietnam had already reached an agreement about who was Laotian and who was Vietnamese. Those who ate short-grain rice, built their houses on stilts, and decorated their homes with Indian-style serpents were considered Laotians. Those who ate long-grain rice, built their houses on the ground, and decorated their homes with Chinese-style dragons were Vietnamese. The kings taxed the people accordingly hence they had no need for boundaries. It was simple; each person belonged to the kingdom whose values they shared and whose king they honoured![11]

Cleansing

Have you ever had mulberry stains on anything? If you get those stains on your favourite white garment you might as well kiss it good-bye. Nothing will get it out again; except, it is said, for green mulberries. And nothing will remove the stain of sin from the human soul except for the blood of Christ.

---

[10] Smith, J.K.A. *Who's Afraid of Postmodernism?*
[11] *Word for Today* 3-1-08

Coffee

You know you're drinking too much coffee when: The nurse needs a scientific calculator to take your pulse. You get a speeding ticket even when you're parked. You grind your coffee beans in your mouth. You watch videos on fast-forward. You lick your coffee pot clean. Your eyes stay open when you sneeze. You can type 60 words a minute with your feet. You can jump-start your car without cables. Your only source of nutrition comes from Sugarine. You don't sweat, you percolate. You've worn out the handle on your favourite coffee mug. You go to AA meetings for the free coffee. You've worn the finish off your coffee table. Starbuck's owns the mortgage on your house. You're so wired you pick up FM radio. You sleep with your eyes open. Instant coffee takes too long.

Commitment

"I never go to church," a man boasted to his ex-pastor. "Maybe you've noticed my absence." "As a matter of fact, I had noticed," said the pastor. "Well, the reason I don't go to church is that there are so many hypocrites there." "Oh, I wouldn't let that stop you from coming," replied the pastor. "There is always room for one more, you know."

Two men fishing on Sunday morning were feeling pretty guilty, especially since the fish didn't bite. One said to the other, "I feel a bit guilty about not being in church. I guess I should have stayed home and gone to the service." The other replied lazily, "I couldn't have gone to church anyway." "Why not?" he asked. "My wife is sick in bed."

41

Have you heard the story of the hen and the hog? They were walking down the street and came to a church with a sign outside: Help The Needy. They started to talk about it. The hen said, "I know how we could help. We could give them ham and eggs for breakfast." The hog was horrified: "That's okay for you. For you it's only a contribution, but for me it's total commitment."

Communication

A man went to his dentist complaining of toothache. She examined him and said, "It's your molar." Looking puzzled, that man asked, "What's a molar?" "It's your six-year molar," she replied. "You'll have to excuse me," said the patient. "But I don't really remember which tooth came through when I was six years old." Her assistant was more in tune. She reached out and poked her finger on the man's cheek near the back of his mouth. "Thanks, that I understand," said the man.

A little old lady and her husband decided to take a holiday in Alabama. Writing to a particular camping group to make reservations in the deep down south of Alabama, she wanted to make sure that the grounds were properly equipped, but felt uncomfortable asking about the toilets. As she felt that the word "toilet" was indelicate, she finally settled on the old-fashioned expression, "bathroom commode." Unfortunately, as she began to write her letter, she still thought the term a little crude. So she began her letter again and decided to abbreviate bathroom commode to B.C. and wrote, "Do the camp grounds have their own B.C.?" The owner of the grounds, not having the same sensitivities as the old lady, had absolutely no idea what a B.C. was. He was completely baffled. After talking it over with some friends, he finally came to the conclusion that B.C. stood for Baptist Church, and so he wrote her the following reply. "Dear Madam, I am happy to advise that the local B.C. is located nine miles north of the grounds and is capable of seating 150 people. I realise that is a fair distance to travel if you are used to going regularly, but most people take their lunches and spend the day there. My wife and I last went about six years ago, and it was so crowded that we spent the whole time standing up. Fortunately, they are planning a fund-raising supper in the basement of the B.C. to raise money to buy new seating. It pains me greatly that I am not able to go more regularly, but it is not due to lack of trying. It just seems that as we grow older, it's more difficult, especially in cold weather. If you decide to stay with us, maybe I could go with you the first time, sit with you and introduce you to all the regulars, because we want you to experience the best we have to offer. The Proprietor."

A Brisbane dad had quite a job trying to fathom the instructions on how to set up the MP3 player on a remote-control car he received for Christmas. It said, "A MP3 wire was collocated in the packing box, unbent pin connecting the player implement, curving pin insert the ORA on the instrument board. When pull out the curing pin, turns to stochastic music."

A British tourist was travelling in California and talking to the American next to her. "Where are you going?" asked the American. "I'm going to San Jose," said the Brit. "That's not quite right," said the American. "In California we pronounce the Js like Hs. So it sounds like Hosay. Have you ever been there before?" "Yes," she replied. "Last Hune and Huly."

I received a letter from my grandmother last week. She is eighty-eight years old and still drives her own car. She writes: Dear Gavin, The other day I went up to our local Christian bookstore and saw a "honk if you love Jesus" bumper sticker. I was feeling particularly sassy that day because I had just come from a thrilling choir performance, followed by a thunderous prayer meeting. So I bought the sticker and put it on my bumper. Boy, I'm glad I did, because what an uplifting experience that followed! I was stopped at a red light at a busy intersection, just lost in thought about the Lord and how good He is, and I didn't notice that the light had changed. It is a good thing that someone else loves Jesus because if he hadn't honked, I'd never have noticed. I found that lots of people love Jesus! Why, while I was sitting there, the guy behind started honking like crazy, and then he leaned out of his window and screamed, "For the love of God! Go! Go! Go!" What an exuberant cheerleader he was for Jesus! Everyone started honking! I just leaned out of my window and I started waving and smiling at all those loving people. I even honked my horn a few times to share in the love. I saw a guy waving in a funny way, with only his middle finger stuck up in the air. I asked your cousin George in the back seat what that meant. He said it was probably a Hawaiian good luck sign or something. Well, I've never met anyone from Hawaii, so I leaned out the window and gave him the good luck sign back. George burst out laughing. Why, even he was enjoying this religious experience! A couple of the people were so caught up in the joy of the moment that they got out of their cars and started walking towards me. I bet they wanted to pray or ask what church I attended, but this is when I noticed the light had changed. So, I waved at all my brothers and sisters grinning, and drove through the intersection. I noticed I was the only car that got through the intersection before the light changed again and felt kind of sad that I had to leave them. After all the love we had shared. So I slowed the car down, leaned out the window and gave them all the Hawaiian good luck sign one last time as I drove away. Praise the Lord for such wonders. Love, Grandma.[12]

A couple of men were out hunting when one of them collapsed and stopped breathing. Panicking, his friend called emergency services on his mobile. "What am I supposed to do?" he blurted. "I think my friend is dead!" The operator replied calmly, "Just relax. First of all, let's just make sure that he's really dead." The phone went quiet, then the operator heard a shot. Then the hunter got back on the line. "Okay, what's next?"

A young city man was visiting relatives on their outback property for the first time. When he arrived, it was a particularly busy time for the farmer. Not wanting to be inhospitable, his uncle said, "Look, we're flat out right now, but why don't you borrow my shotgun and take the dogs out for a bit of shooting." When his nephew returned a couple of hours later, the farmer asked him, "How was the shooting?" "That was amazing," said the young man. "Got any more dogs?"

Compassion

A highwayman had been caught and was convicted of his crime. Waiting to be hanged, he was told by a priest that he was going to go to hell but that it was still not too late to repent. The highwayman looked at him and replied, "You live such comfortable lives, you could not possibly believe in what you believe. If I

---

[12] An email I received.

believed in the hell that you preach, I would crawl the length of England on broken glass just to make one convert."

Competition

Playing table tennis, a father was asked by his young son, "What's the score, Dad?" His father smiled and replied, "Son, for there to be a score, you have to be able to hit them back."

Complacency

Jesus will lift you out of the deepest pit, but He will not lift you out of your armchair. Reinhard Bonnke

Compromise

Don't persecute the Christians or they will become strong and spread. Instead, wherever you find Christians grouped together, build cinemas, drinking halls, night clubs, and gambling dens and they will destroy themselves. Nehru, India's first president.

I don't play in Satan's playground. If I played in his playground, he'd eat my lunch. Paul Ruzinsky

Computers

Three reasons dogs don't use computers: 1. They can't stick their heads out of Windows Vista. 2. They have an irresistible urge to attack the screen when they hear, "You've got mail." 3. The saliva-coated mouse is difficult to manoeuvre.

Confession

A picture on a postcard shows two goldfish in a bowl. One is whistling and looking outward. The other says, "Don't try to hide it. I can see the bubbles."

When going to confession, young children at a Catholic school often forgot what sins they were supposed to confess, so the priest suggested that the students make lists. The following week, one child went to confession with his sins written on a scrap of paper. He began, "I talked back to my parents. I lied to my teacher. I punched my brother and..." His voice trailed off. Then he said in an angry voice, "Hey, this isn't my list!"

Confidence

A professor faced his class of molecular biology students who were waiting nervously to take their final exam. He said, "I know how hard you have all worked this semester in preparation for this test, and that you all have great plans for the future. You have studied well, and I am certain that you will all pass this exam. Therefore, I am willing to give an automatic B to anyone who decides not to sit for this test." Immediately, a bunch of students jumped to their feet, thanked the professor, and left. "Anyone else want to leave?" asked the lecturer. "I won't offer again." Another student packed up and left the room. The professor then handed out the test. The few remaining students stared at the page before them. It said, "Well done. You have been awarded an A for this subject. Always believe in yourself."

I do not boast that God is on my side. I humbly pray that I am on God's side. Abraham Lincoln

Conflict

When you see someone driving towards you on your side of the road, and they're drunk, doing 130kmh, and swerving all over the place, you don't just think, "Well, I'm sober and doing the speed limit. I'm in the right; let them move." Paul Newsham

Conscience

A head hunter may have no conscience about scalping a man from another tribe, but may feel guilty about killing a monkey, because he has been taught that monkeys are sacred.

God put a secret agent inside of you; his name is conscience. Peter Youngren, on the conscience's function to confirm the preaching of God's Word.

A conscience is what hurts when all your other parts feel so good.

A clear conscience is usually the sign of a bad memory.

Contentment

Once upon a time, there was a king who was dying and whose wise men advised him that if he covered himself with the shirt of a contented man, he would be completely healed. The king immediately sent his men throughout the entire kingdom hoping to find a contented man. Finally, after many months of searching, they returned empty-handed. "What!" said the king. "Was there no one in my kingdom who is contented?" "Yes, Your Majesty," they replied. "We found one man." "Then where is the shirt?" asked the king. "Your Majesty, he had no shirt." Contentment has nothing to do with what you have, but everything to do with what you are.

Sometimes you don't know that Jesus is all you need until Jesus is all you've got. Wayne Cordeiro

We were driving along on a country road, checking out the beautiful scenery. What caught my eye was the sight of four horses eating near each other. Two were on one side of a fence, and another two on the other side. What amused me was that they all had their heads poking through the fence and were eating the grass on the other side! They seemed just a like a lot of people I've met; never quite happy with what they've got.

Discontent robs a man of the power to enjoy what he possesses. A drop or two of vinegar will sour a whole glass of wine. T. Watson

It's 8 am, there's a knock on the door, and a guy gives you $100. You ask, "Why are you giving this to me?" He replies, "I just wanted to share it." That evening you're telling everyone. Next day at 8 am, there's the same guy knocking on your door and handing you $100. This happens every day for three weeks, and by then you're just waiting at the door. By the end of the seventh week, you're leaving an envelope at the door with a note scrawled on it: Leave money here. After three months, you go out and check the envelope and there's nothing there. The same thing happens the next day. On the third day, you're waiting at the door, and you see the guy walk past your place to your neighbour's house. "Hey, that's the wrong house," you yell. The next day it's the same. You shout, "Hey, he doesn't deserve that. What are you giving him the money for?" Eventually, you become angry and resentful that you are no longer getting something you didn't deserve in the first place. You took it all for granted. In the beginning, the sense of privilege was very high, but over time it diminished. You stopped being thankful and became susceptible to discontent.

A businessman was on vacation in Mexico. Relaxing on the beach, and staring out over the water, he watched a fisherman haul his boat ashore. "That's a lot of fish," he said admiringly. "How long you been out there?" "Not long," said the fisherman. "So how do you spend the rest of your time?" he asked. "I play with my children, read a little, take a siesta with my wife, Christina. Then at night, our *amigos* come over and we play cards and drink wine." "Well," said the businessman, "You're talking to the right person. I studied business at Harvard. My advice to you is: Stay out fishing for longer, sell all your excess fish, buy more boats, build your own cannery, and move to New York to run your business." "How long would that take, *señor*?" "Probably about twenty years." "Then what happens?" "Then it's time to put your company on the stock market and make millions of dollars." "And then what do I do, *señor*?" "Then you can retire. Just think, you could play with your children, read a little, take a siesta with your wife, get your friends over each night, play cards, and drink wine."

Conversion

Conversion is like changing your car from petrol to rocket fuel. You've changed from one source of power to another. But it's still a car.

Cooperation

Geese fly in a V-shaped formation when they fly south for the winter. Apparently, the V-shape enables geese to fly at least 71% farther than if they were flying solo. The reason for this is that each bird causes an updraft for the goose behind, which makes flying much easier. Geese that fall out of formation experience wind resistance that slows them down. They need to rejoin the formation as quickly as possible, otherwise they will be unable to keep up with the rest of the flock.

I remember years ago hearing about two churches that united into one. But do you think they understood the real meaning of unity and cooperation? The two formerly different churches would assemble on two different sides of their hall and they'd sing their songs at two different tempos!

Counselling

A man went to a counsellor for advice. His marriage was really bad and he wanted out, but he wanted to hurt his wife as much as possible. The counsellor thought for a while, then said, "I have an idea. This is the way to really hurt her. For the next three months, treat her like a princess. Love her, bring her flowers, buy her gifts, take her out to dinner, do some of the housework. Treat her like she's the most wonderful woman in the world. Then suddenly, you just leave. That'll really kill her." So he did. A few months later the counsellor saw the man walking and said, "So how's bachelor life treating you?" "What do you mean?" asked the man. "You know," said the counsellor. "How'd it go when you dumped your wife?" Looking perplexed, the man replied, "You've got to be kidding. I'm married to the most wonderful woman in the world." The counsellor walked away smiling to himself.

Courage

Courage is not the absence of fear, but rather the judgement that something else is more important than fear. Ambrose Redmoon

Jesus didn't come to make us safe; He came to make us brave.

Any old dead fish can float down stream, but it takes a live fish to float upstream.

In 1852, the troopship *Birkenhead* struck a sunken rock off the African coast. As well as the troops, there were 124 women and children on board, and there was only room for them in the lifeboats. The men lined up and watched without a sound as the lifeboats shoved off. Major Seton gave the order, "Stand still, and die like Englishmen." And that's what they did, all 454 men. I wonder what those men felt as they watched the lifeboats pushing off. I wonder how many of them were tempted to race up to the major and say, "But major, I'm only 22 years old. Are you sure there isn't room for just one more?" They might have felt like it, but they didn't do it. As they went down with the ship, they overcame their fear with raw courage.

True courage is not the absence of fear, but the mastery of fear. Mark Twain

When my daughter was around 13 years old, she was talking to some of her friends and referred to her mother as "Mummy." One of the young guys in his twenties said incredulously, "Mummy?" She looked up at him and said, "Yeah, you got a problem with that?" The smirk disappeared, and he immediately backed down mumbling, "Er, no." Sometimes all it takes is a bit of courage.

Creation

According to one website, there are probably about 400 billion stars in our galaxy, and the way to estimate the number of stars in the universe is to multiply that number by the number of galaxies. The Hubble telescope is capable of detecting about 80 billion galaxies. So multiply 400 billion by 80 billion and you've got an approximate answer. Psalm 147:4 He counts the number of the stars; He calls them all by name.

Crime

A bandit who robbed a bank in Tulsa, Oklahoma, told the teller: "Don't do anything stupid, lady." Then he fled, leaving his hold-up note … a pre-printed withdrawal slip with his name on it. He should have taken his own advice.

Student Jan Michael Ihl was charged with theft after plugging his laptop into a socket of a railway station in Germany and stealing electricity worth less than five cents.

Criticism

If there was any real power in criticism, the skunk would have been extinct years ago. Mark Twain.

Mary was well-known as a critical person. One day, she was asked what she thought of Sue, a woman she barely knew. "I don't like her," she commented. "She keeps changing her mind. Every time I ask her the time, she gives me a different answer."

A young girl went to her pastor and confessed that she feared she had committed the sin of vanity. "What makes you think that?" asked the minister. "Because every morning when I look into the mirror I think how beautiful I am." "Never fear, my girl," was the reassuring reply. "That isn't a sin, it's only a mistake."

The only reason they put you up front, is so they can see clearly enough to shoot at you. Paul Newsham

A young man was visiting his parents during the university holidays. When his father discovered that he had only just scraped a pass in one of his core subjects, he commented, "That's not very good, is it?" The young man replied, "Dad, I learned something really important in my communication studies. If you have something negative to say, you should use what's called the 'feedback sandwich.'" "And what's that?" asked his father. "First, you say something positive, then the negative comment, then finish with another positive comment. Do you understand what I mean?" "Yeah, I think so," said the father. "How's this for size? I love you. Put a sock in it. I love you."

It's interesting how the best soccer players in the world aren't shooting goals in the World Cup. They are sitting up in the stalls yelling, "Hey, you should have ..."

Crucifixion

Dead people don't get offended.

A woman's husband liked baked dinners, chocolate, pavlova and percolated coffee. One night, his wife decided to bless him and serve all his favourite foods for dinner. She prepared a beautiful meal, took it through to where he was sitting in his armchair, watching TV, but he made no response. He showed no sign of being interested in the main meal, the chocolate, the pavlova, or the coffee. Reason? He was dead. The Bible teaches that we are all under the power of the sin virus, but that if we die, it has no more power over us. See Romans 6:6 and Galatians 2:20.

Crying

Women cry on average 64 times a year, and men only 17.[13]

Cuddling

If a baby is startled fresh from the womb, German paediatrician Ernst Moro discovered in 1918, its arms

---

[13] *Reader's Digest* July 2006 p 31

will fly up and out, then come together in a desperate clutch. Holding is good, and floating free is bad – a lesson that's not so much learned after birth as preloaded at the factory. In fact, doctors have long known that babies who aren't held simply fail to thrive.[14]

Cults

One of the biggest hindrances to Jehovah's Witnesses being set free and coming to Christ, is the number of people who snarl at them, "I'm a Christian, I'm not interested." and then slam the door in their face. Ask yourself, if you'd knocked on 3,000 doors, and 95% of the ones who called themselves Christians acted like that, how would you feel about so-called Christians?

Culture

A 500 year-old frozen man was found. They discovered that he had eaten berries, and when they put them in a Petrie dish, the seeds began to sprout. Life was still in the seeds, and all they had to do was change the culture and they started to grow.

Culture is a powerful thing. My wife was talking to the owner of a local fruit shop, and I chimed in and asked his name. "Iz Bruno, mate," he said with a strong Italian accent mixed with a good Australian endearment. Not wanting to miss an opportunity, I put on my best Italian accent and said jokingly, "Bruno, my name's Antonio." He said, "Antonio, where you from, mate?" I said, "Australia. What about you? What part of Italy you from?" He said, "I'm not from Italy. I'm born and bred in Australia, in Tully." As it turns out, Tully, a small Australian

---

[14] *Time Magazine* 19th January, 2004, p47

outback town, has such a high percentage of Italians, that even those born and raised there still speak with an Italian accent.

Death

It is possible to provide security against other ills, but as far as death is concerned, we men live in a city without walls. Epicurus (Ancient Greek philosopher)

The certainty of death and the uncertainty of the hour of death is a source of grief throughout our life. Edgar Morin, French philosopher

When Julio Ruibal, a pastor in Cali, Colombia received death threats from the drug lords, he said, "I am immortal until I've done everything God has asked me to do." He was right, and he preached the gospel fearlessly till he was martyred.

A wealthy young man was told that he needed to turn to God. He dismissed the idea. That night he woke up to find a frightening being at the end of his bed. "Who are you?" he cried. "I am the angel of death." "Is my time up?" "Not yet," said the angel. "Before I come to take you, I will send my messengers to warn you that your time is near." Then the angel disappeared. Relieved, the man fell asleep. The years went by, and he thought, "I've got plenty of time to make my peace with God. There have been no messengers." "That night he woke to find the angel of death sitting on the end of his bed again. "W-what are you doing here?" he stammered. "I've come for you," replied the angel. "But you can't. I mean, I'm not ready." "Well, I've kept my part of the bargain. I sent my messengers." "What messengers?" "How could you miss them? Your grey hair, your wrinkles, your failing eyesight."

One patient said to another, "Are you getting a new suit?" "No, why?" asked the second patient. "Because there was a whole bunch of people measuring you up while you were asleep."

Tragically, three friends die in a car crash, and they find themselves at the gates of heaven. Before entering, they are each asked a question by St. Peter. "When you are in your casket, and friends and family are mourning your death, what would you like to hear them say about you?" asks St. Peter. The first guy says, "I would like to hear them say that I was a great doctor in my time, and a great family man." The second guy says, "I would like to hear that I was a wonderful husband and school teacher who made a huge difference to our children of tomorrow." The last guy replies, "I would like to hear them say ... Look! He's moving!"

When they're dying, people pray about (or think about) what's important. They're not thinking about whether the garbage was put out. In John 17, Jesus prayed about things that were important to Him. What did He pray for? Community in the church.

It was very late in the evening, and after a night of solid drinking, Jack decided to take a short cut through the local cemetery and fell into a freshly dug grave. Unable to climb out, he laid down at the bottom and fell asleep. Early in the morning, the gravedigger heard moaning and groaning, so he went to investigate. When he looked into the grave, he saw Jack shivering and demanded, "What on earth is wrong with you, making all that noise?" "I'm freezing to death," Jack replied. "Well, of course you are," said the gravedigger. "You've kicked all the dirt off yourself."

57

If ancient custom is followed, the Chamberlain will tap the dead pope with a silver hammer and ask: "Are you there?" after a doctor has pronounced John Paul dead. Only then can death be officially recognised.[15]

Sticker on a vehicle with highly polished chrome and clearly someone's favourite toy: "Is there life after death? Touch this ute and find out."

Deception

In China, parents of twin boys hoped to save money on their sons' education, so they sent one twin to school on odd days and the other on evens. The teachers figured it out after six months.

Rat poison: 99.99% good food.

Currency lads (sons of early Australian convicts) used to have fun with the early settlers fresh from England: "When the kookaburra's laughter rang through the trees, a local would grab the new chum's arm and croak, 'Did you hear that? Don't worry, it's only old Joe, the black fella. He eats people, you know – he comes out at sunset. If you hear him in the bush, just come running into the streets yelling and we'll see what we can do to help you.'"[16]

I remember seeing the picture (in *Time Magazine*, May 19th, 2003) of presidential hopeful John Edwards kneeling, holding the hand of a little girl and looking up intently into her face, surrounded by TV cameras and other onlookers. The caption could have read: I must find out what this little girl thinks of where America's headed. Cameras? What cameras? Oh, those! I hadn't noticed.

---

[15] *Sunday Mail* 3-4-05 on the death of a Pope John Paul:
[16] Garvin, Mal *Us Aussies* p31

The US Treasury Department has a special group of people whose job it is to track down counterfeiters. They are not trained by spending hours examining counterfeit money. Rather, they study *the real thing*.

Self-deception: A man bought a new Jeep Grand Cherokee, and to celebrate, he and his four friends drank a lot of beer and went duck hunting. They got the hunting dog, guns, decoys, dynamite, more beer, and drove onto the frozen lake. First they had to blow a hole in the ice for the decoys, but it was too risky to plant the dynamite and run for it. They might slip over. So they decided to toss the dynamite. The Jeep owner felt he was the best thrower, so he walked out a few metres, lit the fuse, and threw it as hard as he could. Now, remember the hunting dog? Born, bred and trained to retrieve, he tore off after it as soon as the stick left his master's hand. Five men yelled frantically at the dog, but the dog ignored them, grabbed the stick, and headed back, tail wagging. His master got his gun and shot at the dog, but couldn't stop the dog with duck shot. Realising that his master was totally insane, the dog ran for cover – under the Jeep Cherokee. Moments later, there was an explosion, and the dog and the Jeep sank to the bottom of the lake.

Baboons are inquisitive creatures. In order to catch one in the Kalahari Desert, the bushman digs a hole in solid rock large enough for a baboon's hand to pass through while extended. He does this while making sure the baboon is watching. Then he drops in some nuts. The baboon is so curious that after the man has gone, he goes to the rock to investigate and puts his hand in the hole to get the nuts. Once his hand is in the hole, the bushman runs to catch him, because as much as the baboon wants to escape he will not let go of what's in his hand, and he cannot get his clenched fist back through the hole. The bushman then feeds the baboon salt, making him extra thirsty. As soon as the baboon is released, he leads the bushman to water.

Decisions

Who you are today is decided by what you chose yesterday. For example, you might want to get into medical school, and you might make a brilliant doctor, but you can't because you chose to play basketball instead of studying.

A man had been made the president of a bank at a relatively young age. Not feeling that confident, he went to see the elderly chairman of the board for some advice. "How can I succeed as president?" he asked. "By making the right decisions," replied the chairman. "But how do I make the right decisions?" "Experience." "But that's precisely my problem. I don't have much experience. How do I get the experience so I can make the right decisions?" "By making the wrong decisions."

Definitions

Adult: a person who has stopped growing at both ends and is now growing in the middle.

Cannibal: Someone who is fed up with people.

Chickens: The only creatures you eat before they are born and after they are dead.

Depression: Anger without enthusiasm.

Dust: Mud with the juice squeezed out.

Egotist: Someone who is usually me-deep in conversation.

Gossip: A person who will never tell a lie if the truth will do more damage.

Inflation: Cutting money in half without damaging the paper.

Secret: Something you tell to one person at a time.

Delegation

Studies have shown that leaders fail because of poor delegation more than from any other cause.[17]

Depression

The US FDA has approved a Prozac-type drug for depressed dogs. This is good, because it's hard for dogs to get therapy; they're never allowed on the couch.[18]

Destiny

One day, climbing through the mountains, a boy found an egg in an eagle's nest. Returning home, he placed it under a hen next to her other eggs. It wasn't so long till the eagle hatched, but surrounded by chickens, he thought he was just another chicken. So he acted like a chicken and scratched in the yard with all the other chicks. He had no idea that he was really an eagle. Occasionally, he felt the desire to do things that chickens don't normally do, but he ignored it. Because a chicken should act like a chicken. One day, he saw an eagle flying overhead. Just then, he knew that he wanted to be just like that eagle. He wanted to be able to fly. He spread his wings and felt the wind in his feathers. Suddenly, he was overcome with the desire to do something no other chicken had

---

[17] *Ministry Advantage, Organising and Delegating* p45

[18] Colin Quinn on Saturday Night Live as quoted in *Reader's Digest* October, 2006 p 41

ever done before; fly off to the distant mountains. He flapped his wings, and as he did, he began to leave the ground. All the other chickens watched as he rose higher and higher into the sky. He had discovered his true destiny.

Details

A man who claimed that he'd swallowed a horse was referred to a psychiatrist who recommended surgery. Collaborating with the surgeon, they decided to bring a horse into the operating room so that when the man woke up he'd think the operation had succeeded. But when he regained consciousness, the man opened his eyes and exclaimed, "That's not the horse I swallowed. It's white. The one I swallowed was black!"

Sherlock Holmes and Dr Watson went out camping together. After a hearty meal, they fell asleep but sometime during the night, Holmes awoke. "Watson," he said, nudging his friend. "Look up and tell me what you can see." "I can see millions of stars," replied Watson. "Why?" "What does that tell you, Watson?" asked Holmes. "Astronomically, it means that there are millions of galaxies with perhaps billions of planets. Horologically, I calculate that the time is about three o'clock. Astrologically, I notice that Saturn is in Leo. Theologically, I can see that God is infinite and that we are insignificant. Meteorologically, I think that tomorrow will be a beautiful day. So what does it tell you, Holmes?" "Watson, you fool. Someone has stolen our tent."

Diligence

Remember Me? I'm the fellow who goes into a restaurant, sits down patiently and waits while the waitresses do everything but take my order. I'm the fellow who goes into a department store and stands quietly while the sales clerks finish their little chit-chat. I'm the man who drives into a petrol station and never blows his horn, but waits patiently while the attendant finishes reading his comic book. Yes, you might say I'm a good guy, but do you know who else I am? I'm the fellow who never comes back, and it amuses me to see you spending thousands of dollars every year to get me back when I was there in the first place and all you had to do was to show me a little courtesy.

Work tirelessly and never give up. John Wesley

Disagreement

If you really want the last word in an argument try saying, "I guess you're right."

There are often two ways of looking at the same set of facts. A teacher took a worm and dropped it in a glass of beer. It died. Then she took another worm and dropped it in some orange juice. It swam around and jumped out of the glass and raced out of the classroom at 100 miles per hour. The teacher asked Johnny, "What does that show?" He replied, "If you've got worms you should drink beer."

Someone once said, "Well, I'll agree that you're right, it means so much more to you than it does to me."

Disappointment

Mary Kay Ash died in 2001 aged 83. She was a "flashy, home-spun cosmetics executive who helped push Mary Kay Inc. to sales of more than $1.2 billion last year".... "She started her company in 1963 with $5,000, after her male assistant at a direct-sales company was promoted at twice her salary. 'I couldn't believe God meant a woman's brain to bring 50c on the dollar,' she said. Famously generous, Ash rewarded her loyal sales force of 40,000 with minks, diamonds and her trademark pink Cadillacs."[19]

Discipline

Bertrand Russell said one reason Hitler lost World War 2 was that he did not fully understand the situation. Bearers of bad news were punished. Soon no one dared tell him the truth. Not knowing the truth, he could not act appropriately.

If you have appendicitis, then you go to the doctor and he prescribes a course of medication. If the medication doesn't work, then the next step is for the problem area of the body (for example, the appendix) to be removed so as not to destroy the whole body.

God's discipline: It's not contradictory to fear a God of love. My children understood a little of what it meant. They understood that the Daddy who kissed and cuddled and tickled them, and bought them chocolate and ice-creams, was the same Daddy who smacked their bottoms when they needed it.

Most of us don't like some foods. When I get a meal like that, I eat the things I least like first. The rest comes easy. There's always enough room for dessert. It's not easy maintaining your motivation when all you've got left to do is the unpleasant stuff.

Someone wrote this about Arnold Schwarzenegger: "On location, a gym goes with him and the work out schedule remains the same. He told me: 'Anyone who wants to be their best, to look their best, must work at it. There are no shortcuts.'"[20]

---

[19] *Time Magazine* December 3, 2001 p22
[20] *Sunday Mail* 28-6-92

Be aware that the pain of discipline will cost you pennies, whereas the pain of regret can cost you millions.[21]

Discouragement

In December 1940, Major General Richard O'Connor attacked the Italian army stationed in Egypt. What made this so extraordinary was that the British had comparatively few troops whereas the Italians had 250,000 men there. O'Connor attacked anyway and had fewer than 2,000 casualties. In the process they destroyed 10 Italian divisions, took 170,000 prisoners and captured 400 tanks and 850 guns – one of the most remarkable feats of arms in history. The decisive factor in the Italian loss was their low morale – because they weren't happy with the alliance with Germany, and they certainly weren't prepared to die for Mussolini. So they broke and retreated at a crucial moment. Discouragement was the key.

Divorce

Court Transcript: Judge: "Well, sir, I have reviewed this case and I've decided to give your wife $775 a week." Husband: "That's fair, Your Honour. I'll try to send her a few bucks myself."[22]

A woman came home, screeching her car into the driveway, and ran into the house. She slammed the door and shouted at the top of her lungs, "Honey, pack your bags. I won the lottery!" The husband said, "Oh, my gosh! What should I pack, beach stuff or mountain stuff?" "Doesn't matter," she said. "Just get out!"

---

[21] Cordeiro, Wayne *Attitudes That Attract Success* p132

[22] *Journal of Court Reporting Online* as described by *Australian Reader's Digest* February 2004 p138

A pastor once said, "If I wanted to get rid of my wife, the most acceptable way in some churches would be for me to kill her. If I divorced her, I could never be a pastor. If I murdered her, I could go to jail, and when I came out, those same churches who would not ordain a divorced man, would welcome me with open arms, and say, 'Wow, what a testimony of God's grace!'"

Doubt And Unbelief

The devil had a closing down sale and was selling all his tools and devices of destruction. Someone asked him how much he wanted for the wedge of doubt. He said, "It's not for sale. I can get back into business with that anytime."

Education

Back in John Wesley's time, laymen were encouraged to preach sermons even though they were not well educated. Using Luke 19:21 – I feared You, because You are an austere man – as his text, and not understanding the meaning of the word "austere," one man thought the Scripture was talking about "an oyster man." He carefully explained how an oyster diver would cut his hands on the jagged shells as he groped in the cold, dark water to retrieve oysters. He talked about how he would then return to the surface holding the oyster "in his torn and bleeding hands." He then explained how Jesus came from heaven to this sinful world "in order to retrieve humans and bring them back up with Him to the glory of heaven. His torn and bleeding hands are a sign of the value He has placed on the object of His quest." At the end of the sermon, twelve men gave their lives to Christ. Later that evening a man approached Wesley grumbling about uneducated preachers who did not understand the Scriptures they were preaching about.

Wesley, educated at Oxford University replied, "Never mind. The Lord got a dozen oysters tonight."

Emergencies

Dispatcher: 9-1-1. What is your emergency? Caller: I have heard what sounded like gunshots coming from the brown house on the corner. Dispatcher: Do you have an address? Caller: No, I'm wearing a blouse and slacks. Why?

Dispatcher: 9-1-1. What is your emergency? Caller: My wife is pregnant and her contractions are only two minutes apart. Dispatcher: Is this her first child? Caller: No, you idiot. This is her husband.

Emotions

Emotions are so unpredictable, they are not a great thing to base your life on. A family emigrated from the UK and went to Australia, but had to leave their goldfish behind with the grandparents. Every week, the grandmother would run a bath and let the fish go for a swim. One time, she ran the bath and put the goldfish in and it went nuts, splashing around and jumping out of the water. She couldn't stop laughing. She called her husband, "Bob, come and have a look at this silly goldfish." He ran in and had a look and said, "Of course he's jumping in and out of the water you silly woman. You've run the hot water." That's when she started to cry. Funny how quickly our emotions can change.

There is some evidence to suggest that if you assume a smile then your physiology follows and you become happier and less able to be angry.[23]

---

[23] De Bono, Edward *Six Thinking Hats* p 18

Encouragement

When you're up, the team needs you; when you're down, you need the team.

A famous singer was to perform at the Grand Opera House. The concert hall was packed. Suddenly the house manager announced, "Ladies and gentlemen I regret that due to illness our special guest will be unable to perform this evening. But we've found another singer, an equally great talent, so would you please give her a warm welcome." The crowd groaned so loudly that nobody even heard the singer's name. You could feel the disappointment everywhere. The stand-in singer gave it everything she had, but when it was over all she got was brief scattered applause followed by uncomfortable silence. Suddenly in the balcony a child stood up and shouted, "Mommy, I think you're wonderful!" Realising what had happened, the crowd jumped to their feet and gave her a standing ovation that lasted for several minutes.[24]

Enthusiasm

Adolph Hitler was a lunatic, but he was an enthusiastic lunatic. That's how he could move people. Duane Vanderklok

Tend to the fire because it's in the nature of fire to go out. William Booth

Abraham is out on the back porch watching the cricket on TV. He dozes off for an hour or two, because you can do that watching cricket and not miss anything. And when he wakes up he sees three men. But he's spiritually sensitive, and senses that this is a visitation from God – what theologians call a

---

[24] *Word for Today* 9-1-08

theophany. He jumps to his feet, runs over to them, invites them to lunch, runs back to Sarah and tells her to make some cakes quickly, then runs to the herd. He selects a calf and tells his servant to hurry to get it ready for lunch. At 99 years old, where did he get all that energy? He got excited because God turned up at his place. One of the wealthiest men of his time, Abraham had stacks of gold and silver and herds, but what made him enthusiastic was when the Lord turned up. (Genesis 18:1-7)

Envy

We were driving along on a country road, checking out the beautiful scenery. What caught my eye was the sight of four horses eating near each other. Two were on one side of a fence, and another two on the other side. What amused me was that they all had their heads poking through the fence and were eating the grass on the other side! They seemed just a like a lot of people I've met; never quite happy with what they've got.

Evangelism

Salt is no good in a salt shaker.

The supreme purpose of every true Christian Church, the chief duty of every Christian minister, the main responsibility of every Christian layman, is to present to all who may be reached, in the clearest and most forceful way, the basic facts of the gospel of Christ, and to urge all who hear to make the definite personal response to these facts which God requires. To this, the supreme task, every other duty and activity of the church, must be secondary and subsidiary. Derek Prince.

Take a man out of the slums, heal his body, give him decent clothes, provide him a home in the country, then let him die and go to hell? ... Really it is not worth it. William Booth

The work of conversion is the first and great thing we must drive at; after this we must labour with all our might. Richard Baxter, Puritan Leader (1615-1691)

The current population of the Soviet Union is 275 million. Only 5% of that number is registered as communist party members. How is it that only 5% of 275 million determine the destiny of so many? We read in the Scriptures how a few dedicated disciples of Jesus Christ turned their world upside down. In similar vein today, the communists, fired with dedication and fervour march on, encroaching systematically into all countries and every area of life. Who will win this power struggle? According to this letter written by a communist, the Red Army will. "The gospel of Jesus Christ is a much more powerful weapon for the renewal of society than is our Marxist doctrine. All the same, it is we who will finally beat you. We are only a handful and you Christians are numbered by the millions. But if you remember the story of Gideon and his 300 companions you will understand why I am right. We communists do not play with words. Of our salaries and wages we keep only what is strictly necessary and we give the rest for propaganda purposes. To this propaganda we also consecrate all our free time and part of our holidays. You Christians, however, give only a little time and hardly any money for the spreading of the gospel of Christ. How can anyone believe in the supreme value of the gospel if you do not practise it? If you do not spread it? And if you sacrifice neither time nor money? Believe me, it is we who will win, for we believe in our communist message and we are ready to sacrifice everything, even our lives. But you, you Christians, are afraid to soil your hands."

If the leading feature of your character is not the absorbing thought and effort to reconcile men to God, you have not the root of the matter in you. Whatever appearance of religion you may have, you lack the leading and fundamental characteristic of true piety – the character and aims of Jesus and His disciples. Look at them and see how this feature stands out, in strong and eternal relief, as the leading characteristic, the prominent design, and the objective of their lives. Charles G. Finney.

Now it came to pass that a group existed who called themselves fishermen. And, lo, there were many fish in waters all around. Streams and lakes were filled with fish, and they were all very hungry. Week after week, month after month, year after year, people who called themselves fishermen met in meetings and talked about their call to fish, the abundance of fish, and how they really should go fishing. They built large buildings for local fishing headquarters, and issued pleas on a regular basis for more fishermen. But they didn't fish. They organised a board to send out fishermen to other places where there were many fish. Their great vision and courage to speak out about fishing were seen in their promotional brochures and spirited rallies to wish these fishermen well. But the staff and committee members just never got around to fishing. Large, elaborate training centres were built to teach fishermen how to fish. Persons with doctorates in "fishology" were hired to do the teaching. They did teach, but they didn't fish. After one stirring meeting on the "The Necessity Of Fishing," one young fellow left the meeting and went fishing. He caught two outstanding fish. He was honoured for his excellent catch and scheduled to visit all the big meetings, to tell about his experience. So he quit fishing to travel about telling his story. Now there were people around them who questioned their status as fishermen, and laughed at their clubs and rallies, when there was never any evidence of any fish being brought in. But they continued claiming to be fishermen, even if they never found time to fish. And Jesus said, "Follow Me, and I will make you fishers of men." Matthew 4:19[25]

Why does the church have a missions department? Does the hospital have a medical department? Or a law firm, a legal department?

A pastor related how his son was in a soccer team that lost every match. He was talking to another soccer Dad and asked him what he did. He was a transport worker. He asked the pastor what he did, so he told him. The man was complaining about their lack of success as a soccer team. The pastor said, "My wife's an intercessor." He said he'd get her to pray that they'd make the finals if the man would come to church when they did. They not only made the finals but won the trophy. The following week, the soccer Dad went to church, and he and his wife gave their lives to Christ.

As we shook hands and bade each other farewell at the end of the seminar, he looked me straight in the eyes, gripped my hand firmly, and said, "Andrew, when they kill me, it will be for speaking, not for being silent." When, not if.[26]

---

[25] *Acts News*
[26] Brother Andrew *The Muslim Challenge* p10

I need partners who aren't on the beach drinking lattés while I'm working my tail off trying to catch fish. Shaun Hansen

Late one night, John Wesley was riding across Hounslow Heath singing a hymn, when someone grabbed his horse's bridle and shouted, "Halt!". The man then demanded, "Your money or your life." Wesley emptied his pockets of the small amount of money he had, then showed the robber his saddlebags which were filled with books. The robber was about to leave when Wesley said, "Stop! I have something more to give you." The highwayman turned back towards Wesley and Wesley said, "My friend, you may live to regret this sort of a life in which you are engaged. If you ever do, I beseech you to remember this, 'The blood of Jesus Christ, God's Son, cleanses us from all sin.'" The robber hurried away. Many years later, people were gathered round to greet the aged Wesley who had just preached at their evening church service. One man in particular wanted to speak with him. Wesley discovered that it was the highwayman of Hounslow Heath many years before. He had become a Christian and was now a successful tradesman. He raised Wesley's hand to his lips, kissed it, and said, "To you, dear sir, I owe it all." "No, no, my friend," replied Wesley. "Not to me, but to the precious blood of Christ which cleanses us from all sin."

A highwayman had been caught and was convicted of his crime. Waiting to be hanged, he was told by a priest that he was going to go to hell but that it was still not too late to repent. The highwayman looked at him and replied, "You live such comfortable lives, you could not possibly believe in what you believe. If I believed in the hell that you preach, I would crawl the length of England on broken glass just to make one convert."

A north Queensland fisherman had a reputation for bringing back huge catches *all* the time. One day, the ranger went with him to see how he was doing it. The fisherman lit a stick of dynamite and threw it into the lake, sending dead fish to the surface. "You can't do that," said the ranger, starting to write out a ticket. The fisherman lit another stick, threw it into his lap and said, "Now, are you going to write out that ticket? Or are you going to join me fishing?"

James Berry (1852-1913) was an English hangman for eight years, in which time killed 134 men and women. His profession took its toll on him and he became a heavy drinker and constantly irritable. Aged 52, while sitting at a station, a young man walked up to him and started to talk to him. He invited Berry to the mission hall where he gave his life to the Lord. Berry became an evangelist till he died aged 61.

Jesus has spent 30 years in preparation for His public ministry. And when He embarked on that public ministry, what did He do? Did He give a seminar on how to build a better marriage? Did He plant a church? Did He start a Bible college? No! He began to preach the Gospel of the Kingdom. Mark 1:14-15

Sinners are not our enemies, they're our targets. Mark T. Barclay

There was a famine in Samaria. The attacking Syrians fled when God caused them to hear the sound of a great army, leaving all their belongings. Four leprous men went to the Syrian camp and found it deserted. They ate and drank and took some of the silver, gold and clothing. Finally, they realised that it was a day of rejoicing and they couldn't keep the blessing to themselves. With a sense of urgency, they told the gatekeepers of the city. (2 Kings 7: 1-10)

Robert Arthington was a 19th century English businessman from a wealthy family. As he was unable to go to the mission field himself, he enabled others to reach the lost by living on a shoestring and sacrificially giving over £500,000 to foreign missions. He wrote, "Gladly would I make the floor my bed, a box my chair, and another box my table, rather than that men should perish for the want of knowledge of Christ."

I prefer my method of evangelism to your method of not evangelising. D. L. Moody

Instead of catching fish, we're trying to build fish tanks.

How shall I feel at the judgment, if multitudes of missed opportunities pass before me in full review, and all my excuses prove to be disguises of my cowardice and pride? W.E. Sangster

Back in John Wesley's time, laymen were encouraged to preach sermons even though they were not well educated. Using Luke 19:21 – I feared You, because You are an austere man – as his text, and not understanding the meaning of the word "austere," one man thought the Scripture was talking about "an oyster man." He carefully explained how an oyster diver would cut his hands on the jagged shells as he groped in the cold, dark water to retrieve oysters. He talked about how he would then return to the surface holding the oyster "in his torn and bleeding hands." He then explained how Jesus came from heaven to this sinful world "in order to retrieve humans and bring them back up with Him to the glory of heaven. His torn and bleeding hands are a sign of the value He has placed on the object of His quest." At the end of the sermon, twelve men gave their lives to Christ. Later that evening a man approached Wesley grumbling about uneducated preachers who did not understand the Scriptures they were preaching about. Wesley, educated at Oxford University replied, "Never mind. The Lord got a dozen oysters tonight."

Evolution

A visitor to a museum pointed to the reconstructed skeleton of a *Tyrannosaurus Rex*. "How old are those bones?" he asked the security guard. "Seventy million, five years and three months old," said the guard. "How can you be so precise?" asked the man. "Easy, those bones were seventy million years old when I started working here. And that was five years and three months ago.

The Monkeys' Viewpoint:
Three monkeys sat in a coconut tree,
Discussing things as they're said to be;
Said one to the others: "Now listen you two.
There's a certain rumour that can't be true,

That man descends from our noble race.
The very idea is a disgrace;
No monkey ever deserted his wife,
Starved her babies and ruined her life,

And you've never known a mother monk,
To leave her babies with others to bunk,
Or pass them on from one to another,
Till they scarcely know who is their mother.

And another thing you'll never see...
A monk build a fence round a coconut tree,

76

And let the coconuts go to waste;
Forbidding all other monks a taste;

Why, if I'd put a fence around the tree,
Starvation would force you to steal from me.
Here's another thing a monk won't do –
Go out all night and get on the stew,

Or use a gun or club or knife,
To take some other monkey's life.
Yes, man descended, the ornery cuss,
But brother, he didn't descend from us." Anonymous

Back in 1925, an evolutionist stated at the Tennessee Scopes Trial, that there were no less than 180 vestigial structures in the human body. They believed that all of those structures no longer served a useful purpose, but were leftovers of the evolutionary process. Today we know better. That list has shrunk to almost zero. Even the mysterious appendix is now known to help produce antibodies and prevent bacteria in the colon reaching the blood stream.

Excellence

You can't learn about excellence by studying failure. If you study bad and invert it, you get not bad.

If a person sweeps streets for a living, they should sweep them as Michelangelo painted, as Beethoven composed, and as Shakespeare wrote. Martin Luther King

Excuses

One Sunday morning, a cop in a small town was `parked at the kerb when he saw a car swerving all over the road. Taking off in hot pursuit, he pulled the driver over, and recognised him as an alcoholic named Frank. The policeman said, "Frank, you're driving all over the place." Frank said, "I'm just trying to get to church, man." Noticing a bottle on the seat next to Frank, the cop asked, "What's that on your seat, Frank?" "It's just water," said Frank. "Give it to me," the cop demanded. He took a whiff. "That's not water," he said. "That's wine." Frank just looked up to heaven and said, "Wow, He did it again."

Experience

Experience alone is insufficient. Napoleon once remarked that if experience was all that was necessary, then his horse would be a great general.

Experience is something you don't get until just after you need it.

Failure

Once, when Mark Twain was asked the difference between a mistake and a blunder, he replied, "If you walk into a restaurant and walk out with someone's silk umbrella and leave your own cotton one, that is a mistake. But if you pick up someone's cotton umbrella instead of your own silk one, that is a blunder."

Better try to do something,
And fail in the deed,
Than try to do nothing,
And always succeed.[27]

Jack Dempsey, former world heavyweight boxing champion said, "A champion is one who gets up when he can't."

If you put a wall-eyed pike in an aquarium with some minnows, it won't be long before you have no minnows. But if you separate the pike and the minnows with a sheet of glass, the pike will charge

---

[27] *The Bible Friend*

them and bounce off the glass. Gradually, over a period of time, the pike learns its lesson. It charges more slowly and less often, till it finally decides that the minnows are untouchable. If you then remove the glass, the pike will starve to death even though it has plenty of food swimming around it. It has finally given up.

Charlie Chaplin once came third in a Charlie Chaplin look-alike competition.

Faith And Works

God said, "This is My beloved Son, in whom I am well pleased," before Jesus did any great works or any miracles.

Having faith is like throwing a pebble into a pond. You can't throw it in without creating little ripples. If there are no ripples that's evidence that there was no pebble in the first place.

A man went looking at real estate. The current owners realised that the property didn't look that good and assured him that they would do it up before he took possession. "Forget it," he said. "I don't want the building. I want the site." God isn't interested in our trying to fix up the building before we come to Him. He's interested in the site. Then He can build whatever He wants on it.

A package from England was sent to a South African town by express. But the man to whom it was addressed refused to pay the delivery charge, and was therefore unable to take possession of it. So for about fourteen years the box served as a footstool in the express office. When the man died, the box was eventually auctioned along with other unclaimed items. There was little interest in the package, but one man bid a low price out of curiosity. When he unpacked the box, he was amazed to find it contained several thousand pounds sterling cash. The original recipient had refused to pay a small delivery charge, and so had missed out on a considerable sum.

You might have a toy dog. It looks like a dog, it's shaped like a dog, it's even got a label on it saying that it's a dog. But it won't bark, play, eat, fetch, lie down and roll over. This is all evidence that it's not the real thing – it's just a lifeless imitation.

Every time a man implements a new idea, he finds ten men who thought of it before he did. Trouble is, they only thought of it.

Faithfulness

Texas National Guard magazine reports the motto of the parachute riggers: I will be sure always. They have to jump the chutes they pack.

Over a 54 year period, John Wesley preached three sermons a day, totalling almost 60,000 times. He travelled by horseback and carriage more than 200,000 miles, knew 10 languages, published grammar books on English, Greek, Hebrew, Latin, and French, seven volumes of sermons and controversial papers, a four-volume commentary on the Bible, an English dictionary, three works on medicine, five volumes on natural philosophy, four volumes on church history, histories of England and Rome, six volumes of church music, edited a library of fifty books, got up at 4 am, and worked through to 10 pm. *Are you getting tired?* Despite all this, he said, "I have more hours of private retirement than any man in England." At 83, he was disappointed that he was unable to write more than fifteen hours a day without hurting his eyes. On his 85th birthday he wrote that he did not feel tired while preaching or travelling. But at 86, he was embarrassed that he could no longer preach more than twice a day. He complained in his diary that he increasingly tended to sleep in till 5:30 am.

Faith In God

A man was walking on a pitch black night when he fell over a cliff. On the way down, he managed to grab hold of a small tree sprouting out of the side of the precipice. Desperately he began to call out for help and a voice answered, "What do you want?" "I'm stuck down here holding on to a tree." He replied. "I can't hold on too much longer. Can you help me?" "Yes," came the reply. "Who are you?" the man asked. "I'm God," replied the voice. "What do you want me to do?" asked the man. "Let go of the tree." For a while there was silence. Then the man called out and said, "Is there anyone else up there?"

A man was caught in a flood, sitting on the roof of his house, and praying and trusting the Lord. After a while, a rowing boat came by and its owner offered him a lift. The man said, "No thanks. I'm trusting in God." Next a helicopter came and he gave the same reply. Eventually the man drowned. When he stood before the Lord, he said, "Lord, why didn't you save me? I trusted You." The Lord said, "I sent you a boat. Then I sent you a helicopter. What more did you want?"

There are two kinds of people. One kind of person looks at a problem and says, "It can't be done". The other kind of person looks at the opportunity and says, "If it could be done how would we do it?"

People criticise Peter for sinking in the water, but at least he got out of the boat.

Spurgeon said, "By faith the walls of Jericho fell down. By faith the walls of this church will be pushed back." Later, the deacons took him to task, telling him that he was presumptuous, since he was only a young man. But during his ministry the walls were pushed back three times.

A man had a dog named Ben. Ben could run around as much as he liked – on a runner. Every so often he'd see a cat and tore off after it, until the sudden yank at the end of the chain. Ben stopped dead. He could go no further. A lot of Christians are like Ben. They put themselves on a runner. An opportunity comes along, something they'd really like to do for God, and they really want to go for it. But yank, it's as if their unbelief says, "This far and no further." Have faith!

Faith is the bucket of power lowered by the rope of prayer into the well of God's abundance. What we bring up depends upon what we let down. We have every encouragement to use a big bucket. Virginia Whitman

Faith Perspective

Each morning, a woman walked to her front gate and shouted, "Praise the Lord!" And each time the atheist next door would yell back, "There is no Lord!" One day she prayed, "Lord, I'm hungry. Please send me some food." The following morning, she discovered a big bag of groceries on her front porch. "Praise the Lord," she shouted. Suddenly, her neighbour jumped from behind a bush. "I told you there was no Lord," he said. "I bought those groceries for you." "Praise the Lord!" the woman said. "He not only sent me groceries, He made the devil pay for them."

If your problems are looking big, and your God is looking small, then you're looking at God through the wrong end of the binoculars.

Two frogs fell into a can of cream,
Or so I've heard it told;
The sides of the can were shiny and steep,
The cream was deep and cold.
"O, what's the use?" croaked No. 1.
"'Tis fate; no help's around.
Goodbye, my friends! Goodbye, sad world!"
And weeping still, he drowned.
But Number 2, of sterner stuff,
Dog-paddled in surprise,
The while he wiped his creamy face
And dried his creamy eyes.
"I'll swim awhile, at least," he said –
Or so I've heard he said;
"It really wouldn't help the world
If one more frog were dead."
An hour or two he kicked and swam,
Not once he stopped to mutter,
But kicked and kicked and swam and kicked,
Then hopped out, via butter!   T.C. Hamlet

When you use a magnifying glass, it doesn't change the size of what you look at. It changes your perception. Dwayne Vanderklok, talking about magnifying the Lord

A man wanted to be a salesman, but he stuttered very badly. Then he saw an ad for a job as a Bible salesman for the Bible Society, and he decided to apply for it because he believed God would help him to do it. At the interview, they heard him stutter and said, "We're sorry, but there's no way you could do this job with that kind of stutter." "Please," he said. "Just give me a chance." They asked him to leave the room so they could discuss it. When he had gone, one of them said, "I have an idea. Let's just give him fifty Bibles and leave him to it. It'll take him years to sell them." So that's what they did. A week later, the man returned. "I've sold them. Can I have some more." Just at that moment the Executive was in session, so they asked him to come in and explain how he'd done it. "Easy," he said. "I just ask them, 'Would you like to buy a Bible, or would you like me to read it to you?'"

Some people have such a big devil and such a little Jesus. Peter Youngren

A scientist was once asked, "What's the result of massive hurricanes on the east coast?" He replied, "New beaches."

Two shoe salesmen arrived on an island. The first one looked around and saw that the natives wore no shoes, and thought, "Why'd they send me here? There's no market for shoes here!" The second one looked around and saw that the natives wore no shoes, and thought, "Wow! Everybody needs shoes – and the whole market is mine."

Fame

A celebrity is a person who works hard all his life to become known, then wears dark glasses to avoid being recognised. Fred Allen

Family

They pamper their children with everything money can buy, from expensive education to a first step on the property ladder. But wealthy parents get a poor return on their investment. The more money spent on children, the less likely they are to enjoy close relationships with their parents as adults, a study found. They move farther away from home, visit their parents less often and make fewer phone calls. Even if they live close to the family home, they see less of their parents than those who are given less, according to the UK study by Essex University's Institute of Social and Economic Research. Professor John Ermisch, who led the study, says material wealth is a poor substitute for love and care.[28]

Almost 75% of young Australians rank family relationships in their top three things most valued, followed by friendships, then physical and mental health.[29]

Fathers & Fatherhood

Whatever your gifting is, if it isn't mixed with the spirit of fatherhood, then your ministry is likely to be a baseball bat. Bill Hilbig

My father used to play with my brother and me in the yard. Mother would come out and say, "You're tearing up the grass." "We are not raising grass," Dad would reply. "We are raising boys." Harmon Killebrew

Ten Things Dad Will Never Say: 1. Well, how about that? I'm lost! Looks like we'll have to stop and ask for directions. 2. Here's a credit card and the keys to my new car ... Go crazy! 3. I noticed that all your friends have certain "get nicked" attitudes. I like that. 4. No son of mine is going to live under this roof without an earring. Now quit your whinging and let's go hang at the shops. 5. What do you want to get a job for? I make plenty of money for you to spend. 6. I don't know what's wrong with your car. Probably one of those doo-hickey thingies that make it run or

---

[28] *Sunday Mail* 3-10-04 p 57
[29] *Reader's Digest* March 2009, p 17

something. Just get it towed to the mechanic and pay whatever he wants. 7. You know pumpkin, now that you are thirteen, you'll be ready for unchaperoned dates soon. Won't that be fun? 8. What do you mean you want to play football? Isn't figure skating good enough? 9. Your mum and I are going away for the weekend. You might want to consider throwing a party. 10. Father's Day, aahh, don't worry about it. It's no big deal.[30]

Tie a boy to a good man, and he almost never goes wrong.

Fear

General George Patton of World War 2 fame was once asked if he ever experienced fear. "Just before an important engagement and sometimes during a battle. But," he added, "I never take counsel of my fears."

Humans are much more dangerous to sharks, which tend to end up in soup or medicine. Fishing nets tangle and drown about 100 million sharks each year. In California there is only one shark attack for every 1 million surfing days, according to the Surfrider Foundation. You are 30 times as likely to be killed by lightning. Poorly wired Christmas trees claim more victims than sharks, according to Australian researchers. And dogs – man's best friends – bite many thousands more people than sharks do.[31]

I only worry on Wednesdays. Any other day I have a worry I write it down and put it in a box. By the time I get to Wednesday I find most of the worries have

---

[30] *North Lakes Messenger*
[31] *Time Magazine* July 30, 2001, p 44

been taken care of. J. Arthur Rank – one of the world's major movie producers.

Unusual fears: Ophthalmophobia – fear of being stared at; Arachibutyrophobia – fear of peanut butter sticking to the roof of the mouth; Paraskavedekatriaphobia – fear of Friday 13th; Genuphobia – fear of knees; Pogonophobia – fear of beards; Alektorophobia – fear of chickens; Coulrophobia – fear of clowns; Dendrophobia – fear of trees; Didaskaleinophobia – fear of going to school; Hippopotomonstrosesquippedaliophobia – fear of long words; Thanatophobia – fear of death; Athazagoraphobia – fear of being forgotten or ignored; Ochlophobia – fear of crowds; Nyctophobia – fear of darkness; Scopophobia – fear of being looked at by other people; Kakorrhaphiophobia – fear of failure; Monophobia – fear of loneliness; Gamophobia – fear of marriage; Peniaphobia – fear of poverty; Hypengyophobia – fear of responsibility; Categelophobia – fear of being made fun of; Schoolphobia – fear of school; Theophobia – fear of God; Hadephobia – fear of Hell.

What happens if you get scared half to death...twice?

It's common for the last words of pilots before a crash to be mostly swearing because of fear.

Fear causes sickness: And Moab was exceedingly afraid of the people because they were many, and Moab was sick with dread because of the children of Israel. (Numbers 22:3)

An Indian fable talks about a mouse that was constantly in fear of a cat. So one day, a magician changed the mouse into a cat. But then the cat was afraid of a dog. So the magician changed the cat into a dog. But the dog was afraid of a tiger. So the magician changed the dog into a tiger. But then the tiger was afraid of a hunter. Finally, in exasperation, the magician said, "Be a mouse again, you have only the heart of a mouse and I cannot help you."

A man said to his wife just before an important engagement, "I'm so nervous, I've got sweaty palms and a dry mouth." His wife replied, "Then why don't you lick your palms?"

Fellowship

Ten Reasons Why I Never Wash. 1. I was made to wash as a child. 2. People who wash are hypocrites – they reckon they're cleaner than other people. 3. There are so many different kinds of soap. I could never decide which one was right. 4. I used to wash, but it got boring so I stopped. 5. I still wash on special occasions like Christmas and Easter. 6. None of my friends wash. 7. I'm still young. When I'm older and have got a bit dirtier, I might start washing. 8. I really don't have time. 9. The bathroom is never warm enough. 10. People who make soap are only after your money. If this puzzles you, don't worry. The same reasons are given by people who don't attend a Christian fellowship. The tragedy is those people actually believe their reasons are valid.

Not everyone has to have close fellowship with every other member of the body of Christ. It's a good thing that your nose and your armpit don't have close fellowship.

Flexibility

Acts 17:22-34 When Paul was in Athens, he saw an altar with the inscription: "To the unknown God." He even quoted one of their poets. He was flexible enough to begin with what they knew and he led them into what they didn't know, allowing the Spirit of God to do His work. But read his sermon, he didn't quote Scripture once.

Focus

In May 1954, Roger Bannister became the first man ever to run a mile in under four minutes. The following month, Australian John Landy shaved another 1.4 seconds off his record. A showdown was inevitable, and in August, the two athletes raced in Vancouver, Canada. By the time they got to the last lap, Bannister and Landy were well in front of the other runners, with Landy in the lead. It seemed certain he would win. But as he approached the finish line, Landy could not help wondering how close behind Bannister was. His need to know was so strong that he couldn't resist the temptation to look over his shoulder. And just as he did, he lost his stride. At that point, Bannister took the lead and won the race. Later, Landy said, "If I hadn't looked back, I would have won the race."

When you focus on something, peripheral vision is blurred. Focus on Jesus so that everything else in your peripheral vision is blurred by comparison.

One morning, a six-year-old girl missed her school bus. Being new to the neighbourhood, her father agreed to drive her to school as long as she gave him directions. They spent twenty minutes going round in circles, but finally arrived at the school, which was only a few blocks away from their home. "Why did you take us all over the place when your school is so close to home?" asked her exasperated father. "Because this is the way the school bus goes," she replied. "I don't know any other way."

Food

Obesity accounts for 280,000 deaths each year in the U.S. alone. If current trends continue, the battle of the bulge will overtake smoking as the primary cause of preventable death.[32]

Never eat more than you can lift. Miss Piggy

Fish and chips has been voted Britain's favourite food of all time, beating roast beef and Yorkshire pudding, roast lamb and mint sauce, and bangers and mash.[33]

Some women were meeting together in a weight-loss group. An older woman was losing lots of weight and was asked by one of the younger women how she did it. "Easy," she replied. "I just take my teeth out every evening at six."

Every year, Australians throw away 3.3 million tonnes of food – a quarter of the nation's tucker [food] supplies.[34]

Foolishness

On 3rd February, 1990, in the US, a man apparently attempted to commit armed robbery. Unfortunately, he made five foolish mistakes. 1. His target was a gun shop. 2. The shop contained a number of firearms customers in a state where a large percentage of the adult population are permitted to carry concealed handguns. 3. He had to walk around a marked police car to get into the shop. 4. A uniformed officer was standing at the counter. 5. The man announced a holdup and began firing his gun, at which point the policeman and the attendant shot him,

---

[32] *Time Magazine* 19th January, 2004, p94

[33] *Reader's Digest* May 2006 p 18

[34] *Reader's Digest* July 2005 p 16

covered by several customers who had also drawn their guns.

Forgetting

A parent sent this note to school to explain their daughter's absence: "Please excuse Sophie for being away from school yesterday. We forgot to get the Sunday paper off our front lawn, and when we saw it there on Monday, we thought it was actually Sunday."

Forgiveness

A psychology student said to his father, "One thing we learn in psychology is how to deal with people's guilt. We try to convince them they shouldn't feel guilty. But no matter how much we try it doesn't work." His father was a Christian and said, "Son, of course it doesn't work. They *are* guilty."

Ps 103:12 "As far as the east is from the west, so far has He removed our transgressions from us." God said He has removed our sins as far as the east is from the west. Why not as far as the north is from the south? Because you can only travel north for a limited distance. Once you hit a certain point, you will be going south again. But it doesn't matter how far east or west you travel, you will still be travelling east or west.

Evangelist Charles Finney preached on 1 John 1:7: "....The blood of Jesus Christ His Son cleanses us from all sin." A stranger who had been in the service asked Finney to walk home with him. Leading Finney into the rear of a building, he locked the door and pocketed the key. "Don't be afraid," the man said. "I just want to ask a few questions. Do you believe what you preached tonight?" "I most certainly do," replied Finney. The man explained that they were in the back of a saloon and that he was the owner. Mothers would come to the saloon, place their babies on the counter, and beg him not to sell liquor to their husbands. "I turn a deaf ear to their cry. When a man leaves here we make sure that he's well and truly under the influence. More than one man has died on the railway tracks after leaving here. Can God forgive a man like me?" the man asked. "I have but one authority. 'The blood of Jesus Christ His Son cleanses us from all sin,'" said the evangelist. The stranger wasn't satisfied yet and asked, "If a man doesn't spend all his money on liquor, we take him to our gambling hall and fleece him of his last dollar with marked cards. Can God forgive a man with a heart like that?" "I have only one authority. 'The blood of Jesus Christ His Son cleanses us from all sin,'" Finney replied again. The stranger still wasn't finished. He said, "Across the street is my wife and daughter. Neither has heard a kind word from me in five years. Their bodies bear the marks of my brutal attacks. Can God forgive a man with a heart like that?" Finney lowered his head and said, "You've painted one of the darkest pictures I've ever seen. But still I have only one authority. 'The blood of Jesus Christ His Son cleanses us from all sin.'" That night that man became a new creature in Christ, quit his business, and began to treat his family with kindness.

People who say they don't want to go to church because they went once and someone hurt them, are like the person with diarrhoea who says, "I had a bad experience in a toilet once, and I'll never darken the door of a toilet again."

Bitterness is like drinking poison and waiting for the other guy to die.

A Christian soldier ended every day by praying and reading his Bible. Each night, he knelt by his bunk while the others looked on. Usually, there was some ridicule, but one night as he knelt in prayer, one soldier threw his boots and struck him in the face. Everyone expected a fight, but the Christian did not retaliate. The following morning, the soldier who threw his boots was surprised to find that they had been polished and placed at the end of his bed.

There's no revenge as complete as forgiveness.

Foundations

The Twin Towers in Kuala Lumpur were (as at October 2002) the tallest buildings in the world, standing at 452 metres. Each tower weighs 300,000 tons. The foundation consisted of a 4.5 metre thick raft foundation containing 13,200 cubic metres of reinforced concrete, weighing approximately 32,550 tonnes under each tower. The bigger the building, the stronger the foundation needs to be.

Friendship

48% of parents on Facebook have "friended" their children.[35]

If Barbie is so popular, why do you have to buy her friends?

I destroy my enemies when I make them my friends. Abraham Lincoln

Every business is built on friendship. J.C. Penney

Future

Faulty predictions: Law will be simplified [over the next century]. Lawyers will have diminished, and their

[35] *Reader's Digest* December 2010. P 18

fees will have been vastly curtailed. (Journalist Junius Henri Browne 1893) By 1960, work will be limited to three hours a day. (John Langdon-Davies in *A Short History of the Future* 1936) Get rid of the pointed-ears guy. (NBC Executive to Gene Roddenberry, creator of Star Trek, regarding Mr. Spock, 1966)

Fear of the future: 21% of Australians are concerned they may lose their job over the next few months, with almost one-third seeking additional sources of income other than their primary job.[36]

Gifts

One Christmas, when I was a kid, my parents gave me and my brother pedal cars. We were excited. We unwrapped them, opened up the packages, and played for ages – with the boxes. God gives each of us gifts, but many Christians never get any further than the wrapping.

The best dairy cow in the world can't be a race horse. It may be saying, "I'm confessing, I'm believing, I'm gonna win this race." But it's still a dairy cow.

A genius (IQ 160) is in the desert, the nearest water is 200 kilometres away, and his motorbike is broken. A mechanic (IQ 100) fixes the bike. The genius becomes a moron and the mechanic becomes a genius.

Giving & Generosity

An old minister was trying to inspire his unmotivated congregation. He said, "This church must get up and walk." "Amen," a pious looking deacon shouted. "Let her walk." Encouraged by the support, the minister

---

[36] *Reader's Digest* March 2009, p 17

said, "This church must run." "Amen, let her run," said the deacon. "More than that," shouted the preacher, warming to his message, "This church must fly." "Amen," the deacon yelled again. "Let her fly!" The minister was now ready to reveal his plan. He said, "Brethren, it takes money to make a church fly." "Amen," said the deacon. "Let her walk."

John Wesley gave away £30,000 to £40,000 just from sales of his books. That was an amazing achievement for someone who lived in the eighteenth century. When his annual income was £30, he gave £2 to the Lord. The following year, when his salary doubled, he continued to live on £28 and gave the Lord £32. The Lord entrusted him with increasing amounts of money, so that in 1787 he was able to tell one of his preachers that he never gave away less than £1,000 per year.

Now it came to pass that as the time of vacation drew near, a certain church member bethought of sandy beaches by the lake and his wife thought of the mountain. The member spoke and said, "Lo, the hot days come and my work lieth heavy upon me, let us depart and go where fishes do bite, and where the cool winds bring refreshment and the land is beautiful about us." "Thou speakest words of wisdom," said his wife. "Yet three, nay even four things must we do ere we go!" "Three things think I of, but not a fourth," said the husband. "That we ask our neighbour to minister unto our flowers, that we arrange for our grass to be mowed and watered, and that we have our mail forwarded. But no other thing cometh to mind." "The fourth is like unto the other three, but greater than all," said his spouse. "Even this, that thou dip into thy purse and fill thy Church envelopes as thou hast committed thyself, that the good name of the Church may be preserved, that the heart of the Treasurer may be made glad, and that it may be well with thee. For verily I say unto thee, thou hast more money now than thou wilt have when thou dost return from thy vacation!" And the husband replied, "Verily, thou art noble and wise among women." And he did attend unto his envelopes ere he sojourned in the country. And the Treasurer rejoiced saying, "Of a truth, there are those who indeed care for the good of the Church!" And it was so. Anonymous

A very wealthy man was asked to make a donation to the church building fund. The case was made very compellingly, the situation explained, and an appeal was made for his assistance. The man listened to the appeal and said, "Look, I completely understand why you think I can give a hundred thousand dollars to the building fund. I have my own business and, as you've probably noticed, I have all the signs of wealth. But there are some important factors you aren't aware of. For instance, did you know that my mother is in an expensive nursing home?" "Well, no, we didn't know that," replied the churchmen. "Also, did you know that my brother died, and left behind a family of five, and that he had absolutely no insurance?" "No, we didn't know that either." "And did you know that my son is a deeply committed Christian, is working with the poor, and earns less than the national poverty level to support his family?" "No, we didn't." "Well, then, if I don't give any of them a cent, what makes you think I'd give anything to you?"

There are some people who say, "I can only afford to give a little. When God gives me more money, then I'll be more generous." But it doesn't work that way. What would you think of a farmer who said, "I'm not going to plant any corn seeds this year. When God gives me some corn, then I'll plant some seeds." Giving is sowing seeds and you can only reap a harvest if you plant them.

When you give to God, He never spends a cent on Himself.

A successful businessman gave his taxi driver a miserly tip. The driver complained, "Yesterday, I gave your son a ride in my cab and he gave me ten times as much as that!" "My son has a rich father," the businessman replied. "I don't!"

Andrew Carnegie gave away $350 million. He said in his 1889 *Gospel of Wealth* that "the man who dies ... rich dies disgraced."

It was coming up to Christmas and so a barber whose business was booming decided that for the next two weeks he'd give the first customer of each day a free haircut. On the first day, the first customer was a baker. Next morning, he presented the barber with a dozen donuts. On the second day, a florist received a free haircut, and thanked him by placing a dozen roses on his counter. On the third day, it was a preacher. Guess what? The following morning there were a dozen more preachers all waiting for free haircuts!

Three pastors were talking about how they get paid. One said, "I draw a circle on the floor. Then I throw the offering money up in the air. And whatever is inside the circle I keep, and whatever is outside is God's." "I draw a circle on the floor too," said the second. "Then I throw the offering money up in the air. And whatever is outside the circle I keep, and whatever is inside is God's." The third pastor said, "I draw a circle on the floor too. Then I throw the offering money up in the air. And whatever He wants He keeps."

You can't live a perfect day without doing something for someone who will never be able to repay you.
John Wooden

A famous philanthropist was once asked, "How are you able to give so much and still have so much?" "Well," the generous man replied, "as I shovel out, He shovels in and the Lord has a bigger shovel than I have."

On his deathbed, a wealthy, miserly old man called for his wife. "I don't want to leave my money behind. I want to take it all with me," he told her. "So promise me you'll put it in the coffin when I die, every last cent." She promised she would. After the man died, his widow went to the memorial service with a friend. Just as the undertaker was about to close the casket, she put a shoebox inside. Her friend was horrified. She said, "Tell me you didn't put the money in there." "Well, I promised him I would," replied the widow. "So I got it all together, deposited it in my account, and wrote him a cheque. It's in the box, so if he can cash it, he can spend it."

Giving Up

Florence Chadwick, noted for swimming the English Channel in both directions, decided to swim the 21 mile stretch of icy water between Catalina Island and the coast of California. It had never been done by a woman, and at age 34, she was determined to be the first. The chosen date was 4th July, 1952, a holiday, and much of the country was watching on television. At several points during the swim, rifles had to be blasted over the waves to fend off the sharks. After nearly 16 hours in the water, she complained of numbness. She squinted to see the shore, but the fog reduced her visibility to almost zero. She called out to her mother and her trainer in the rescue boat that she couldn't go on. They encouraged her to continue, but when she looked to where she thought the shore should be, she could see nothing. She gave up and was pulled out from the water. Imagine how she felt when she discovered that she was only half a mile from shore. She knew she physically could have done it. Later, she told reporters that she wasn't making excuses for her failure, but "if only I could have seen land, I know I could have made it." She was right. Just a few weeks later she attempted the same swim, under the same foggy conditions, and finished the swim in record time. Not only did she become the first woman to complete the icy stretch, but she beat the men's record by two hours.

Goals

In 1954 a survey was made of individuals graduating from Yale University. It was found that only 3% had definite written financial goals; 10% had a clear idea, but had not written it down; 87% had no idea of their goals. 20 years later, these Yale graduates were again interviewed. The 3% who had written goals had made more money than all the rest combined.

A king was hunting in a forest when he stumbled upon a tree with several targets drawn on its trunk. Right in the centre of each circle was an arrow. "Who is this fine archer?" the king asked his men. "I must find him and recruit him for my army." Just at that moment, a boy carrying a bow and a quiver of arrows walked by. Overhearing the king, he admitted that he was the one who had shot the arrows. "Are you sure you didn't just push the arrows into the middle?" asked the king. "No, sire," said the boy. "I shot them from a hundred paces." "That is amazing!" cried the king. "From now on, consider yourself to be in the service of your king." The boy was overjoyed. "Now, tell me," continued the king, "how did you come to be such an excellent archer?" "Well," said the boy, "first I shoot the arrow at the tree, then I paint a ring around it." [Many people are guilty of setting goals they can't possibly miss.]

God – His Nature, Attributes And Power

There is a story that Newton made an elaborate clockwork model of the solar system. When someone remarked on how clever he was to construct such an intricate mechanism Newton replied that the Good Lord must be a lot cleverer still to have constructed the real thing.[37]

God's Word

A good compass always points to true north, no matter what. God's Word is our life compass. We should use it to make sure that we're pointing in the right direction.

A man goes to the doctor and says, "Doctor, I'm coughing my heart out. It feels like my lungs are burning up." "Let's take a look," says the doctor. So the doctor examines him. "It's not looking good. But you're in luck. I've got a bottle of medicine here. The instructions are on the bottle. It'll clear this up in three days." Five days later the man returns. "Doctor, you told me this stuff would cure me in three days. I'm not getting better. I'm getting worse." "Did you read the instructions?" the doctor asks. "Of course I read the instructions," the man replies. "It says ..." The doctor snatches the bottle out of his hand. "Gimme that

---

[37] Davies, Paul *Superforce*

bottle. This bottle is unopened." "You didn't say I had to open it." "Listen, you came in to see me. I examined you. I diagnosed your problem. I gave you the medicine. Now it's over to you." How many Christians know that God's Word has power to transform their lives, to heal, to deliver, to give wisdom, to counsel, but they just never seem to get around to reading it on a regular basis, and putting it into practice?

If you have time to watch TV or read a novel, a magazine, or a newspaper every day, but don't have time to read God's Word, then you love all these things more than God's Word.

Gospel

A person may sincerely believe their plane won't crash, but their sincerity won't save them if it does. It won't change what actually happens. "Our beliefs – no matter how deeply held – have no effect on reality."[38]

Christianity now has to preach the diagnosis – in itself very bad news – before it can win a hearing for the cure. C.S. Lewis in *The Problem Of Pain*

Imagine you are speeding along – 30ks over the limit. The police pull you up and begin to write out a ticket, when suddenly you cry out, "Hold on officer! I think you ought to know that I made a donation to charity this morning. And not only that, I helped a little old lady cross the road." "Well, I didn't know that," says the policeman. "Why didn't you say so in the first place? Two good deeds and only one bad deed. I think I'll let you go." In reality, the policeman doesn't

[38] Mittelberg, Mark; Strobel, Lee; Hybels, Bill *Becoming A Contagious Christian* p.91

care which laws you've kept; he's still going to book you for the one you broke. No country operates differently from that. Why would we expect God to operate on that basis?

The strongest, richest, most educated man outside the ark was lost. But the weakest, poorest, least educated man in the ark was saved. Reinhard Bonnke

Grace

James Berry (1852-1913) was an English hangman for eight years, in which time killed 134 men and women. His profession took its toll on him and he became a heavy drinker and constantly irritable. Aged 52, while sitting at a station, a young man walked up to him and started to talk to him. He invited Berry to the mission hall where he gave his life to the Lord. Berry became an evangelist till he died aged 61.

A little girl got saved and applied for membership to a church. "Were you a sinner?" she was asked. "Yes," she replied. "Are you still a sinner?" "Yes." "Then what real changes have taken place in your life?" "The best way I can explain," said the little girl, "is that I used to be a sinner running after sin, but now I'm a sinner running away from sin."

The camp director ran the most amazing camps. They were well organised, there were games, sports and everybody had a great time, especially at the Saturday night rally. One boy, Nicky, was from a severely dysfunctional home. He disrupted everything, bullied smaller kids and swore at others. The camp director had an idea. When he shared it with his leaders, they were shocked. He called Nicky in and got him to answer honestly how many stripes of the cane he thought each of his bad deeds was worth. When they had gone through the list, it totalled twenty-five. "You can't cane me that much," said Nicky. "It wouldn't be Christian." "You're right," said the camp director. "I'm not going to cane you twenty-five, or five, or anything." The director took off his shirt and sat on a chair hugging its back. He took all twenty-five, by which time Nicky understood the meaning of grace.

Just before Christmas Day in 1943, in WW2, Charlie Brown – a real person – was 21 years-old, and an American pilot fighting for the British. Charlie had been on a mission to bomb a factory in Germany, but they'd taken a lot of hits. Their B-17 was in a bad way. The nose was smashed, the tail section was shredded, one propeller had stopped working, holes everywhere. And to make matters worse, the compass had stopped working, and instead of heading back to the UK, they were headed deeper into enemy territory. Three of his men were seriously wounded and they were 400 km from Britain. German pilot Franz Stigler was ordered to go up and shoot them down. But when he got up there, he was stunned. He had never seen a plane in such bad condition, and he didn't have the heart to shoot them down. Instead, he signalled for them to turn around, and he escorted them all the way to the North Sea. Then he returned to Germany and told his commanding officer that he'd shot them down over the ocean. It would be 46 years till these two men would meet and that amazing act of grace would become public knowledge.

The grace of God allows you to be someone you're not, and do something you can't. Mark Driscoll

Greatness

Great faith is the product of great fights. Great testimonies are the outcome of great tests. Great triumphs come only from great trials. The highest military decoration in many countries is symbolised by a cross – the sign of the greatest conflict and greatest victory.

Grief

It's not wrong to move to grief; it's just wrong to stay there.

Grief can come for a holiday, but it can't take up residence with you.

Growing Up

Why is psychoanalysis quicker for a man than a woman? Because when it's time to go back to his childhood, he's already there.

Guidance

God either guides with His eye (the look), or with a bit in the mouth. Some Christians wait for the bit.

In Italy, there is a harbour that can only be accessed via a narrow channel lined with dangerous, narrow rocks. In the middle of the night, it is extremely difficult to steer a ship safely through. Maritime authorities recognised the danger and placed three special lights throughout the harbour to guide vessels at night. Captains are not to steer their ships from one light to the next. Instead, each light must be perfectly lined up with each other. If a captain can see separate lights in the distance, he is off course, as all three must line up perfectly. Getting God's guidance is similar. It's important to have confirmation of what you believe God is telling you to do. "Out of the mouth of two or three witnesses..."

When Columbus set out on his journey to America, he didn't know where he was going, when he arrived he didn't know where he was, and when he returned he didn't know where he'd been.

God didn't tell the Israelites the whole plan in one hit for capturing the Promised Land. He just told them to cross the Jordan River. Then, once they'd done that, He told them how to capture Jericho, then how to capture Ai, then the Amorite kings, and so on. It was one step at a time, and it forced them to trust Him.

Guilt

A man lost his wallet. A few days later he received a letter: "Sir, I found your wallet. I feel so guilty that I am returning some of your money. If guilt bothers me any more I shall send some more money."

False guilt: I have offended God and mankind because my work didn't reach the quality it should have. Leonardo da Vinci

A postcard shows two goldfish in a bowl. One is whistling innocently and looking outside. The other says, "Don't try to hide it. I can see the bubbles."

A minister had sinned very badly and even though he had confessed his sin, he never felt forgiven. A lady in his church was always saying, "The Lord said to me ..." It wasn't that he didn't believe her, because she was usually right, but she really irked him. One day he said, "If God is speaking to you, ask Him to tell you what it was I did years ago." A few days later, she came back to him. "Well?" he demanded. "Did you ask Him?" "Yes," she replied. "And what did He say?" asked the minister. "He said He doesn't remember."

The moralities accepted among men may differ – though not, at bottom, so widely as is often claimed – but they all agree in prescribing a behaviour which their adherents fail to practise. All men alike stand condemned, not by alien codes of ethics, but by their own, and all men therefore are conscious of guilt. C.S. Lewis in *The Problem Of Pain*

An apology hotline created by Jesse Jacobs has enabled people to apologise without actually talking to the person they have wronged. They log 30-50 calls each week. Says Jacobs, "The hotline offers participants a chance to alleviate their guilt and, to some degree, to own up to their misdeeds."

Only 11% of women feel guilty about flirting with a friend's partner, compared with 29% of men.[39]

Like Adam, we hide from God. But it's like a child playing hide and seek, facing the wall with their hands over their eyes. They think that no one can see them because they can't see anyone.

When I was at school I remember a teacher telling us of a boy whose nervous system took a long time to tell him of pain. He put his hands on the stove and felt nothing for a while. When he did, it was too late, his hands were stuck. Our sense of guilt is meant to warn us of danger, because sin is dangerous to our spiritual life.

You can't keep blaming yourself. Just blame yourself once, then move on. Homer Simpson

---

[39] *Reader's Digest* November 2009, p 16

Happiness

An old dog was watching a puppy chasing its tail and asked, "Why are you chasing your tail?" The puppy said, "I have mastered philosophy, and I have solved the problems of the universe which no dog has ever before been able to solve. I've learned that the best thing for a dog is happiness, and that happiness is in my tail. Therefore I am chasing it, and when I catch it I shall have it." "My son," said the old dog, "I too have considered the problems of the universe in my weak way, and have formed some opinions. I have also judged that happiness is a fine thing for a dog, and that happiness is in my tail. I've noticed that when I chase it, it just keeps running away from me. But when I go about my business, it follows me wherever I go."

Health & Healing

A patient went to her doctor about a weight-loss patch she'd seen advertised. "Apparently, you stick it on, and the kilos just fall off. Does it work?" she asked. "Sure," the doctor replied. "If you put it over your mouth."

Fear causes sickness: Numbers 22:3 And Moab was exceedingly afraid of the people because they were many, and Moab was sick with dread because of the children of Israel.

A hypochondriac went to a doctor and burst into tears. "I'm certain I've got liver disease, and I'm going to die from it." "That's ridiculous," said the doctor. "You wouldn't even know if you had liver disease or not. There's no discomfort of any kind with that ailment." "That's right!" said the hypochondriac. "And those are my exact symptoms!"

A study of 1,000 Israeli men with heart conditions found that those men who felt they were loved by their wives had a 50 per cent reduction in their angina and cardiac disease.[40]

Hearing (God's Voice)

A woman went to her pastor and said, "A brother has spoken to me and said that the Lord is sending me to Africa." Her pastor replied, "If you go you'd better take that brother with you, otherwise you won't know when to come back, will you?"

Hallmark Father's Day card: "Dad, thanks to your lectures I never change horses in the middle of a job worth doing, I know the squeaky wheel gets the worm, and I never count my chickens until I've walked a mile in their shoes ... And you thought I wasn't listening."

Heart

The distance between heaven and hell is the distance between your head and your heart. Bill Newman.

Heaven And Hell

It was the start of a holiday weekend and the service station was crowded. Finally an attendant hustled up to the local minister who had been waiting in line some time. "I'm sorry for the delay, pastor," he apologised. "Seems like everyone waits until the last minute to get ready for a trip they knew they were going on." "I know what you mean," said the pastor. "I have the same problem in my business."

Latest Travel Information For Heaven: Accommodation: Arrangements for first class accommodation have been made in advance. (John

---

[40] *Reader's Digest* June 2005 p 164

14:2) Passports: Persons seeking entry will not be permitted past the gates without having proper credentials and having their names registered with the ruling Authority. (Rev 21:27) Tickets: Your ticket is a written pledge that guarantees your journey. It should be claimed and its promises kept firmly in mind. (John 5:24) Customs: Only one declaration is required while going through customs. (1 Cor 15:1,3,4) Immigration: All passengers are classified as immigrants, since they are taking up permanent residence in a new country. The quota is unlimited. (Heb 11:16) Luggage: No luggage whatsoever can be taken. (1 Tim 6:7) Air Passage: Travellers going directly by air are advised to watch daily for indications of imminent departure. (1 Thess 4:17) Vaccination/Inoculation: Injections are not needed as diseases are unknown at the destination. (Rev 21:4) Departure Times: The exact date of departure has not been announced. Travellers are advised to be prepared to leave at short notice. (Acts 1:7)[41]

Three men died and went to Heaven. Peter said, "Come on in guys. I've got to show you your homes." The first got a beautiful mansion. So did the second. When it got to the third, he was shown a little grass hut. "What! Is that all I get?" he said. "Sorry pal," replied Peter. "But that's all we could do with the materials you sent up."

The distance between heaven and hell is the distance between your head and your heart. Bill Newman.

Hitting The Mark

The universe is absolutely huge. Even in our local neighbourhood – the Milky Way – distances are

---

[41] *Church News Service*

awesome. For instance, the nearest that Mars ever gets to Earth is 56 million km. So when they want to send a rocket to Mars, they have to calculate everything right down to the smallest fractions. If they send it in a direction only half a degree out, they'll miss Mars altogether. And a miss is a miss whether they miss by 1,000 km or a million km. Life is a little bit like that. A few little changes here and there, a few detours along the way can make the difference between hitting the mark and missing the mark.

Holiness

False Holiness: Simeon was 13 years old, and like many of his contemporaries in the 5th century he thought that the only way he could get closer to God was by punishing his body. So he gave up his job and went into a monastery, but it was too easy. So after trying different things, he found a 60-foot pillar in the wilderness with a platform three feet wide and climbed to the top. His disciples would put food and water in a basket he'd lower down to them. He'd pray and often stand with arms outstretched in the form of a cross, sometimes up to eight hours at a time. Other times he'd bow over and over again, almost touching the platform with his head. Once he did it 1,240 times before he collapsed on the platform. He remained on the platform, in all kinds of weather, for 37 years!

Holy Spirit: His Work And Fruit

Conviction by the Holy Spirit often hurts. It's like being in a dark room for some time and having someone turn on the light. It hurts your eyes.

Coincidences are those moments when God chooses to remain anonymous.

There was a young man who complained that whenever he was filled with the Holy Spirit, he was like a bucket with holes. The Spirit merely drained out of him. His friend said, "That may be true, but even a bucket full of holes can be filled with water if it is immersed in the river and left there."

Mark Twain made enough money to buy his own steam ship. When coming into a town, he would often blow the whistle. He was occasionally known to blow it for so long that he ran out of power, and drifted downstream while the power built up again. Christians are sometimes like that – they use the power of God for themselves (blowing their own whistles), and then when they need it, they don't have enough left.

Cars run on the storage principle – fuel is stored in the vehicle and then it runs out as the vehicle is driven. Electric trains run on the contact principle – they maintain contact with the source of power. Having the Holy Spirit is the contact principle.

Our life is like a house with many rooms. One by one, the Holy Spirit goes into each room and turns on the light. We have a choice. We can either respond and let Him show us what He wants, or we can try to turn off the light and keep Him out of the room. If we keep trying to turn off the light, there will come a point when He will stop trying to turn it on.

Talking about a friend of his, a lecturer at a Bible College related the following story: The Holy Spirit keeps a testimony in different cultures. One missionary went to an African tribe that had had little contact with white people. When he arrived, they were in the middle of a ceremony which was remarkably like our Communion. Because he was a linguist, he was able to understand a lot of what was said. When they got to the end they said, "We do this in memory of Him whose name we cannot remember." He stood up and said, "I want to tell you His name. His name is Jesus."

Duncan Campbell was apparently at a conference when he had a strong feeling to go to the Hebrides. When he arrived, he made his way up to the church where the cleaner was going about his work. "What's happening here?" he asked. "We have a speaker tonight," said the cleaner. "What is his name?" Duncan Campbell inquired. "Duncan Campbell," replied the cleaner. "But I'm Duncan Campbell! How did you know I was coming?" "How did you know to come?"

David Brainard, missionary to the Susquehanna, Delaware and Stockbridge Indians once preached through an intoxicated interpreter who was so drunk he could barely stand. Yet scores were converted through the preaching. Brainard's secret was his prayerfulness.

A Bible college lecturer asked his students to examine all the Scriptures they could find on the Holy Spirit and put their findings in alphabetical order. This is the list they came up with: Acceptance, ability, adoption, anointing, appointments, Boldness, blessing, Cleansing, character, comfort, commands, conviction, confidence, confirmation, counselling, conscience, Deliverance, discernment, discipling, disciplining, deposit, Empowering, enabling, encouraging, Faith, fellowship, freedom, fruit, Gifts, glory, Godhead, goodness grace, grieving, guidance, guarantee, Healing, hope, helping, holiness, Impartation, inspiration, inner witness, interpretation, Joy, judgment, Knowledge, Life, liberty, love, Miracles,

New birth, Obedience, oneness, Peace, perseverance, power, prayer, prophecy, preaching, persuasion, Quickening, Release, revival, revelation, righteousness, Sanctification, the sword, sealing, sonship, strength, Teaching, truth, tongues, Trinity, transformation, Unity, utterances, understanding, Vitality, vindication, victory, Warning, wisdom, witness, X-ray vision, Youthfulness, Zeal

Homosexuality

On the subject of a "gay gene", Alan Chambers, president of Exodus International (ministry to gays), who himself was homosexual till he was transformed by Christ, said, "Who cares if it is genetic? Science should never be used to try to trump God's Word. ... Look, just because something is genetic doesn't make it healthy, optimal, desirable, or right."[42]

A lecturer was trying to explain to a student how deductive reasoning worked. "For instance," he said, "I could reason a lot about you just from one small piece of information." "Really?" said the student. "Yes. Do you have a dog?" "Yes." "Then you'll probably live in a house." "Yes." "Then you'll probably have a family." "Yes." "Then you'll probably have children." "Yes." "Then you're a heterosexual." "Wow. That's amazing." He was so impressed that he decided to try it on his friend." "I could reason a lot about you just from one small piece of information." "Really?" said his friend. "Yes. Do you have a dog?" "No." "What! You're a homosexual?"

Is there a gay gene? Does it matter? What if they found a gene that made someone alcoholic? That

---

[42] Chambers, Alan *God's Grace and the Homosexual Next Door* p 36

113

would not make alcoholism right, and it wouldn't change the fact that God can set that person free.

Honesty

Pepe Rodriguez was one of the most dangerous bank robbers in the wild, wild west. He would sneak over the border into Texas, rob a bank, and then flee back to Mexico. The Texas Rangers got so frustrated they decided that they would cross the border illegally and track him down. There was a long search, and finally they trapped him in a Mexican bar. All the lawmen had their guns drawn. Pepe was terrified. He could speak no English and the Rangers couldn't speak any Spanish. So they asked Pepe's friend, the bartender, to translate. He explained to Pepe who they were. The Rangers asked the barman to tell Pepe that they wanted to know where he had hidden all the money. If he didn't tell them, they would shoot him down like a dog. The bartender translated, and Pepe began to tremble. "Tell them the money is hidden in the well. Count down twelve stones from the top, and that's where all the loot is." The bartender turned to the Rangers and said, "Pepe is not afraid to die. He says that you are a bunch of filthy dogs, and he will never tell you where the money is."

Hope

Shortly before his death, Gandhi wrote, "All about me is darkness; I am praying for light." Contrast this with evangelist D. L. Moody's last recorded words: "This is my triumph; this is my coronation day! It is glorious!"

Humility [See Pride Too]

While men searched for a throne to build their kingdoms, Jesus reached for a towel to wash His disciples' feet.

In Room 41 in London's National Portrait Gallery women flock to see a 1-metre-wide plasma screen showing a 67-minute video of David Beckham – asleep! Entitled *David*, Sam Taylor's video was commissioned by the gallery. All that can be seen is Beckham's shirtless torso.

Humour

A few days before his thirty-ninth birthday, Nelson was in London for his investiture as a Knight of the Bath. The king was there in person and remarked, "You have lost your right arm!" Rarely at a loss for words, Nelson replied, "But not my right hand, as I have the honour of presenting Captain Berry." With that, he pushed forward his delighted junior.

Hurt

People who say they don't want to go to church because they went once and someone hurt them, are like the person with diarrhoea who says, "I had a bad experience in a toilet once, and I'll never darken the door of a toilet again."

Hypocrisy

If you allow the hypocrites to get in between you and God, guess who's closer to God?

Immorality

Coleen Nolan (youngest member of 80s girl band *The Nolans*) "agreed to pay for 18-year-old son Shane to travel to Amsterdam and visit a prostitute as a 'reward' for passing his exams."[43]

---

[43] *Sunday Mail* 12-6-05 p 61

Indwelling

I am His residential address on earth. Reinhard Bonnke

Reinhard Bonnke related the story of how he went into a music store to buy some equipment. After a while the salesman, who had initially ignored him while smoking, came up to him and said, "I can see Jesus in your eyes." Reinhard Bonnke asked God, "How can that happen?" The Lord replied, "Jesus resides in your heart and sometimes He likes to look out of the windows."

Inheritance

Imagine you had a rich uncle who died and left you $1 million. You think, "At last, I'm a millionaire, and I always will be. Nobody can take that away from me." But the minute you got that $1 million, it became subject to the Rule of 72. This is a principle economists use to calculate (among other things) the effects of inflation. You just divide 72 by the inflation rate and that tells you how many years till your money is worth half as much in buying power. So, if you've got $1 million, and the inflation rate is 6%, you divide 72 by six which is twelve. That means that in twelve years time your $1 million will only be able to buy what $500,000 can today. That's inflation. So the effect of inflation is that the money you inherit is always devaluing. But your spiritual inheritance never does. See 1 Peter 1:3-4.

Inspiration

Bill Hybels told this story: He was pitching for his baseball team. His coach emphasised how they were depending on him, and Bill was all pepped up. He got the ball, gave it his best pitch, and just as it left his hand, he realised that his catcher was talking to the umpire. The ball hit the catcher in the chest so hard that he collapsed. They laid him in the dugout. Bill ran over, and the catcher looked at him as if to say, "What were you thinking?" Hybels said, "I was inspired!"

Integrity

Somebody once said that in looking for people to hire, you look for three qualities integrity, intelligence and energy. But if they don't have the first, the other two will kill you. Warren Buffett

A preacher got on a bus and discovered he had been given too much change. When he was getting off the bus, he told the bus driver who replied, "I know." "Why did you give me too much?" asked the preacher. "I was in church yesterday and heard you preach," replied the driver. "I wanted to see if you were worth listening to."

72-year-old Warren Buffett has a personal fortune estimated to be $30.5 billion (U.S.) – "second only to Bill Gates." He "once raised $210,000 at a charity auction for his 20-year-old wallet, with a stock tip inside." This was because of his reputation.[44]

Intelligence

"Don't tell anyone. I'm supposed to be dumb." Danish supermodel and photographer Helena Christensen, disclosing in an interview that she speaks six languages.

A man joined a poker school for the first time and was amazed to see a dog sitting in. He watched as the dog held three cards in his left paw, while drawing two

---

[44] *Time Magazine* 10-3-03 p45

cards with his right. The newcomer said to the dog's owner, "What a wonderful dog. You must be terribly proud of him." The owner replied, "Aw! He's not so smart. Every time he gets a good hand, he wags his tail."

Intentions

"Reverend," said a man to a minister, "I want to make you aware of a family I know who are in terrible need. The parents are both out of work and struggling to raise their six children. They're hungry and will soon be evicted from their home unless someone pays the $3,000 back rent they owe." "How awful!" said the minister, amazed at the concern of the man. "I'll organise a collection. May I ask who you are?" The visitor sobbed, "I'm their landlord."

Inventions

In May 2001, Melbourne man John Keogh successfully obtained a patent on what he called a "circular transportation device." Other people may know it as the wheel. Keogh is a patent lawyer and his move was partly tongue-in-cheek. He wanted to show the flaws in the Australian government's low-cost patenting system.

Joy

Rufus Moseley was once asked did he think that Jesus ever laughed. "I don't know," Moseley said. "But He certainly fixed me up so that I could."

Judging

I still remember the day I bought my first piano. The salesman could not look me directly in the eye, and gave me the distinct impression of being shifty and dishonest. A few years later I was describing him to someone and they said, "Oh, yeah. I know the guy you're talking about. He's the one with the eye problem." "The what?" I asked. "The eye problem. He can't look straight ahead." The man had an eye defect that made it impossible for him to look straight at me. Boy, did I learn a lesson about judging others!

A secluded jungle tribe was being supplied with tinned food. On the first can was a picture of a cow. It contained beef. On the second can was a picture of a corn cob. It contained corn. The third can contained baby food and on the tin was a picture of a baby. What do you think they thought was in the can?

A man in a hot air balloon realised he was lost. He reduced altitude and spotted a man below. He descended a bit more and shouted, "Excuse me, can you help me? I promised a friend I would meet him an hour ago but I don't know where I am." The man below replied, "You are in a hot air balloon, hovering approximately thirty feet above the ground. You are between 40 and 41 degrees north and between 59 and 60 degrees west longitude." "You are obviously a technical person," said the balloonist. "I am," replied the man, "but how did you know?" "Well," answered the balloonist, "everything you told me is technically correct, but I have no idea what to make of your information, and the fact is I am still lost. Frankly, you've not been much help to me at all." The man below responded, "You must be in management." "I am," replied the balloonist, "but how did you know?" "Well," said the man, "you don't know where you are or where you are going. You have risen to where you are due to a large quantity of hot air. You made a promise which you have no idea how to keep, and you expect people beneath you to solve your problems. The fact is you are in exactly the same position you were in before we met, but now, somehow, it's my fault."

A man caught a taxi and discovered that the driver had a Master's degree in psychology. He asked him if it helped him in his job. "Sure it does," replied the taxi driver. "It gives me a real understanding of why some people cut in front of me, or others speed up when I try to pass." Expecting a Freudian analysis, the man asked, "So, why do they?" The taxi driver said, "Because they're jerks!"

The Alarm, a British rock band who hadn't had a hit for more than 15 years, broke back into the charts by releasing a single under a false name. They said that image-obsessed DJs refused to play their music. So they put out their new song, *45RPM,* under the pseudonym of *The Poppyfields*. In one week, it sold 4,000 copies and reached No. 28 in the UK charts. Singer Mike Peters said, "We wanted the song to be judged on its merits."

Ever noticed that anybody going slower than you is an idiot and anyone going faster than you is a maniac? George Carlin

Judgment

A woman who had been on the *Titanic* before it sank said that the people who were on deck were getting pieces of ice from the iceberg, throwing them around, and even putting them in their drinks. People can be so close to judgment or disaster and yet not know.

What do people do when they spot a prairie fire coming? They can't escape on the fastest horse. They take a match, light the grass around them, then they stand in the burned area and are completely safe. They can hear the flames roar around them, but they are unafraid. Why? Because the fire has already passed where they stand and they are in no danger. When the fire of God's judgment comes, you can stand where the fire has already been – in Christ. God's judgment was already passed on Him, on our behalf, when He was crucified. (See Isaiah 53:5-6)

No country in the world allows the keeping of some laws to balance out and pay for the breaking of other laws. In fact this idea could very well encourage people to break the law in "moderate ways". After all, if I go and break one law, I can just go and do something good and then there is no penalty to pay. No country in the world functions in this way, yet we are supposed to believe that a perfect and holy God does.[45]

Justice

In England, a man named Whitefield and his friend were taking five guineas to a widow with a large family. On the way, a highwayman held them up and took their money. Not long after, the highwayman returned, took Whitefield's coat and said, "'Ere, you can 'ave mine." With that, the robber left Whitefield with his. A little later, they heard the highwayman returning, so fearing for their lives, they took off on their horses to the nearest town. When Whitefield took off the coat, there inside was a carefully wrapped parcel with 100 guineas.

Kindness

I was at the local fruit shop and had a few dollars left on me. The lady in front of me started paying for her fruit and vegetables, but found she was 10c short. It's not something I normally do, but I gave her 10c. She

---

[45] E.S. Coplestone *Jesus Christ or Mohammed?* p35

was happy, and the queue moved again. Then it was my turn. Unbelievably, I'd left myself short of 5c when I came to pay, which is not like me at all. For the first time in my life, the lady behind me said, "I've got 5c. Here you go." And so I had enough money to pay for my bananas. The three of us laughed about it. I'd never been part of such a chain of kindness. It made my day. [46] (How sad that the receiving of 5c – an extremely small amount – was the pinnacle of kindness in this lady's experience!)

Shortly before the Battle of Trafalgar, Nelson noticed that his signal lieutenant, John Pasco, appeared to be irritated, and asked him why. Pasco replied, "Nothing that need trouble your Lordship." But Nelson was insistent, so Pasco explained that the bosun who had loaded the mailbags had forgotten to include his own letter to his wife. The ship carrying the mail had already departed for England and was now some distance away under full sail. "Hoist a signal and bring her back," said Nelson. "Who knows that he may not fall in action tomorrow?" The ship returned, and a boat was launched to carry over the single letter. This kindness was remembered by the entire fleet.

Kingdom Of God

In May 1954, Roger Bannister became the first man ever to run a mile in under four minutes. The following month, Australian John Landy shaved another 1.4 seconds off his record. A showdown was inevitable, and in August, the two athletes raced in Vancouver, Canada. By the time they got to the last lap, Bannister and Landy were well in front of the other runners, with Landy in the lead. It seemed

---

[46] Catherine Sies in *Reader's Digest*, July 2007 p 28

certain he would win. But as he approached the finish line, Landy could not help wondering how close behind Bannister was. His need to know was so strong that he couldn't resist the temptation to look over his shoulder. And just as he did, he lost his stride. At that point, Bannister took the lead and won the race. Later, Landy said, "If I hadn't looked back, I would have won the race." (Luke 9:62 But Jesus said to him, "No one, having put his hand to the plow, and looking back, is fit for the kingdom of God.")

The emperor Julian the Apostate (332-63) is reputed to have said ... that he wanted to confiscate Christians' property so that they might all become poor and enter the kingdom of heaven.[47]

In the early gold rush days in Australia in the 1850s, the discovery of gold had a profound effect on our country. It transformed it. People got excited. And in two years the population of Victoria exploded from 77,000 to 540,000. The treasure generated enthusiasm, excitement. That's how it should affect us when we discover the treasure of the Kingdom of God. (Matthew 13:44)

Knowledge

On June 19, 1865, over two years after President Lincoln had signed the Emancipation Proclamation, General Gordon Granger rode into Galveston, Texas, and read General Order Number 3: "The people of Texas are informed that in accordance with a Proclamation from the Executive of the United States, all slaves are free." For the first time, slaves in Texas learned that they were already free. Some were

---

[47] Carson, D.A. *Expositor's Bible Commentary: Matthew 1-12* p132

shocked; many others celebrated. June 19 soon became known as "Juneteenth".[48]

Law and Laws

The law was given to limit retribution. If you walk down the street and punch a guy in the nose, do you think he'd be content to hit you back only once? "An eye for an eye" etc, was not a command, but by way of limitation.

Maybe you heard about the guy who ran stark naked through the city centre shouting, "Politicians are morons!" He was fined $200 for indecent exposure and $500 for breaching the Official Secrets Act.

During the Middle Ages, it wasn't unusual for animals to be tried in courts of law. The prosecutions were based on the Mosaic Law which said, "If an ox gores a man or a woman to death, then the ox shall surely be stoned, and its flesh shall not be eaten; but the owner of the ox shall be acquitted." (Exodus 21:28) Based on this, rats, pigs, horses, and even insects were all taken to court at different times. In 1445, at St. Julien, some beetles were prosecuted for ravaging a vineyard. Unfortunately, the insects didn't attend court, so the case flopped. Even more bizarre, a clothes moth in the 16th century was charged in Spain with destroying a valuable tapestry. Being found guilty, the moth was sentenced to have its throat cut. That was an unfair verdict since, really, its larvae were the guilty parties. In 1314, the French hanged a bull that had gored a man. Then in 1457, a sow and her six young piglets received the death penalty for eating a child. The sow actually was executed, but apparently the piglets were given a second chance on

---

[48] *Our Daily Bread* 19th June, 2008

account of their youth. Humans have passed all sorts of stupid laws – and still do. But there's never been a law against "love, joy, peace, longsuffering, kindness, goodness, faithfulness, gentleness, and self-control."

Three Australians on vacation in Mexico got drunk and woke up in jail. They discovered that they were to be executed, but none of them could remember what they did the night before to deserve the death penalty. The first man, strapped into the electric chair, was asked if he had any last words. He said, "I'm from the Melbourne School of Divinity and I believe that God has the power to intervene on my behalf." When they pulled the switch, nothing happened, so the gaolers decided that God had intervened and let him go. The second man was strapped into the chair and said, "I'm from Queensland University's law faculty and I believe that justice will intervene on behalf of the innocent." Again, the switch was thrown and nothing happened. The guards considered that he too must be innocent and let him go. The last man strapped into the chair said, "I'm an electrical engineer at the University of Technology, Sydney, and you're *never* going to get this thing working if you don't connect those two loose wires."

A lawyer was trying out a creative defence on behalf of his client who was charged with burglary: "My client merely put his arm through the window and took a few items. His arm is not him, so how you can punish a whole man for something his arm did?" "Well said," replied the judge. "If that's the case, I sentence the defendant's arm to one year in jail. If he wants to accompany it, that's up to him." The burglar grinned, removed his artificial arm, placed it on the bench, and walked out of the courtroom.

125

Nowhere is the powerlessness of laws seen more graphically than on the roads. Have you ever noticed how the majority of people on the roads do 70 in 60 zones, 80 in 70 zones, 90 in 80 zones, and anything but 100 in a 100 zone?

If Jesus were here today He would be wanted by: The Liquor Licensing Board for turning water into wine without a licence; the Australian Medical Association for practising medicine without a licence; the Health Department for feeding 5,000 people in the open; the Education Department for teaching without a certificate; the Water Police for walking on water without a life jacket; the RSPCA for driving a herd of pigs into the sea; the Australian Board of Psychiatrists for giving free advice on living a guilt free life; the Women's Liberation Movement for not choosing a woman disciple; and the Inter-Faith Movement for condemning all other religions.

In May 2001, Melbourne man John Keogh successfully obtained a patent on what he called a "circular transportation device." Other people may know it as the wheel. Keogh is a patent lawyer and his move was partly tongue-in-cheek. He wanted to show the flaws in the Australian government's low-cost patenting system.

99% of lawyers give the rest a bad name.

Leadership

An office manager was complaining in their staff meeting that he wasn't getting any respect. The next day, he attached a small sign to his office door: I'm The Boss! Later that day, he returned from lunch to find that somebody had stuck a note over his sign. It read, "Your wife called. She wants her sign back."

A man who became disillusioned with the Apostolic Church backslid. When he came back to the Lord he said, "Apostles are not people at the top holding you down; they are people at the bottom holding you up."

There are five levels of strength: (a) our spiritual ceiling; (b) our emotional ceiling; (c) our mental ceiling; (d) our social ceiling; (e) our physical ceiling. You will rise to the level of your lowest ceiling. Kong Hee

The only reason they put leaders up front, is so they can see clearly enough to shoot at you.

When leaders make a mistake, they say, "I was wrong"; when followers make a mistake, they say, "It wasn't my fault." A leader works harder than a follower and has more time; a follower is always too busy to do what is necessary. A leader goes through a problem; a follower goes around it and never gets past it. A leader makes and keeps commitments; a follower makes and forgets promises. A leader says, "I'm good, but not as good as I ought to be"; a follower says, "I'm not as bad as a lot of other people." Leaders listen; followers just wait until it's their turn to talk. Leaders respect those who are in authority over them and try to learn something from them; followers resent those who are superior to them and try to find chinks in their armour. Leaders feel responsible for more than their job; followers say, "I only work here." A leader says, "There ought to be a better way to do this"; followers say, "That's the way it's always been done here."[49]

The year was 1493. Constantinople was under siege by the troops of Mahomet II. It was about to be

[49] Anonymous as quoted in Watkins, G.F. *G-Men: The Final Strategy* p 99-100

decided whether the Balkans would be under Christian or Islamic rule. Meanwhile, in the besieged city, a local church council was discussing these questions: What gender are the angels? What colour were the holy virgin's eyes? If a fly falls into sanctified water, does the fly become sanctified or the water polluted?

When one of the presidents of the US stated publicly that he didn't like broccoli, there was a big blockade of broccoli growers outside the Whitehouse. Reason? Because they knew that when the President said he didn't like broccoli, sales would fall all over the country.

A good coach knows how to move his players to win the game. A good player knows how to listen to his coach. The pastor is the coach surrounded by all his star players.

You can measure the size of a ship by the size of the wake that it leaves behind.

Studies have shown that leaders fail because of poor delegation more than from any other cause.[50]

1500 pastors leave the ministry every month due to moral failure, spiritual burnout or conflict in their church; 34% of pastors' marriages end up in divorce; 80% of pastors and 84% of pastors' wives feel unqualified and discouraged; 50% of pastors would leave if they could make a living doing something else; 80% of seminary and Bible college graduates will leave ministry within the first 5 years; 80% of pastors believe their ministry affected their families negatively; 33% believed ministry was a hazard to their family; 5% felt themselves unable to meet the

---

[50] Ministry Advantage, *Organising and Delegating* p45

needs of the job; 90% felt inadequately trained to cope with the demands of ministry; 90% work more than 46 hours per week; 70% of pastors feel that they have lower self-esteem now versus when they started out in ministry; 40% of pastors reported having a serious conflict with a parishioner/congregant at least once a month; 70% do not have someone they consider a close friend – someone they can confide in; 37% of pastors confessed to having been involved in inappropriate sexual behaviour with someone in the church; 60% of pastors' wives hold full-time jobs or are involved in careers to meet family needs; 63% suffer marriage problems due to congregational difficulties; 81% suffer marriage problems due to insufficient time together; 94% of pastors felt under pressure to have the "ideal" family; 45% of pastors' wives have no close friends.[51]

In this respect [General] Grant was very much a modern general: he was deeply pained by casualties, and regretted having to order operations that he knew would result in great losses. Nor did he attempt to insulate himself from the men he was ordering into battle. Like the French general Phillipe Pétaine in 1916, and Dwight D. Eisenhower in 1944, he moved among them, giving them the one great gift of which he was capable: confidence that they would prevail.[52]

Learning

Arithmetic test, 1960s: "A logger cuts and sells a truckload of timber for $100. His cost of production is four-fifths of that amount. What is his profit?" New Maths test, 1970s: "A logger exchanges a set (T) of

---

[51] *Willow Magazine* Vol 1, Issue 3, April 2008, p 1-2 citing statistics by George Barna, Victor Parachini & Fuller Institute

[52] Mosier, John *Grant* p103

timber for a set (M) of money. The cardinality of Set M is 100. The Set C of production costs contains 20 fewer points. What cardinality of Set P is profits?" Dumbed-down test, 1980s: "A logger cuts and sells a truckload of timber for $100. His cost is $80; his profit is $20. Find and circle the number 20." New Age test, 1990s: "A logger cuts down a beautiful forest of 100 trees in order to make a $20 profit. Write an essay explaining how you feel about this as a way to make money."[53]

Learning is the prerogative of the learner. Jennie Bickmore-Brand

Legalism

Instructions: Children's medicine: Do not drive car or operate machinery while using this product. On American hairdryer: Do not use while sleeping. Shower cap: Fits one head. Iron: Do not iron clothes while wearing them. Christmas tree: For indoor or outdoor use. Nut packet on American airline: Open packet, eat nuts. Heater: Do not immerse in bath. On a blanket from Taiwan: Not to be used as protection from a tornado. On the bottle-top of a flavoured milk drink: After opening, keep upright. On a British supermarket's tiramisu dessert (printed on bottom of box): Do not turn upside down. On a Swedish chainsaw: Do not attempt to stop chain with your hands or genitals. On frozen dinner: Serving suggestion: defrost. On a dishwasher: Do not allow children to play in the dishwasher. On massage chair: Do not use massage chair without clothing … and never force any body part into the backrest area while the rollers are moving. On flushable toilet brush: Do not use for personal hygiene. On electric

---

[53] *Reader's Digest* July 2006 p 69

hand blender used to blend, whip, chop and dice: Never remove food from blades while the product is operating. On child's scooter: This product moves when used. On a thermometer used to take a person's temperature: Once used rectally, the thermometer should not be used orally. On cat's blanket: Machine washable; remove pet first.

Jesus healed three blind men. One was healed when He touched him. Another was healed when He spoke. Another when He spat in the dirt and made mud. Each blind man started to teach that that was the way to get healed. Eventually they had a conference where they discussed the proper way to be healed. Blind people came to listen, and by the end of the conference they understood each other more. But the blind still went away blind.

Life

Mid-life Crisis: The first half is over and you're at half-time, and you're deciding if you want to play the second half the same as the first half. Mark Ramsay

Listening To God, To Others

When they gave out brains, I thought they said trains and I missed mine. When they passed out looks, I thought they said books and I said I didn't want any. When they passed out noses, I thought they said roses and I ordered a big red one. When they gave out chins, I thought they said gins, and I ordered a double. Boy! Am I a mess!

The word "listen" contains the same letters as "silent". Alfred Brendel

Lordship

A young man joined the Navy, and shortly after asked his officer for a pass so he could attend a wedding.

The officer gave him the pass, but told the new recruit he would have to be back by 7 pm Sunday. "But sir, you don't understand," said the recruit. "I'm in the wedding." "No, *you* don't understand," said the officer. "You're in the Navy!"

Lordship means obedience. If you claim someone is your boss, but don't obey him, he's not really your boss.

God is not an indulgent grandfather who does everything you think He should do. Trevor Chandler

Love

The Pit: A man fell into a pit and couldn't get himself out. A subjective person came along and said, "I feel for you down there." An objective person came along and said, "It's logical that someone would fall down there." A Christian Scientist came along and said, "You only think you are in the pit." A Pharisee said, "Only bad people fall into pits." A news reporter wanted the exclusive story on his pit. A fundamentalist said, "You deserve your pit." Confucius said, "If you would have listened to me, you would not be in that pit." Buddha said, "Your pit is only a state of mind." A realist said, "That's a pit!" A scientist calculated the pressure necessary (lbs. / sq. in.) to get him out of the pit. A geologist told him to appreciate the rock strata in the pit. A tax man asked if he was paying taxes on the pit. The Council Inspector asked if he had a permit to dig a pit. An evasive person came along and avoided the subject of his pit altogether. A self-pitying person said, "You haven't seen *my* pit!" A charismatic said, "Just confess that you're not in a pit." An optimist said, "Things could have been worse." A pessimist said,

"Things will get worse." And Jesus, seeing the man, took him by the hand and lifted him out of the pit.[54]

The knowledge of the father's love did not cause the prodigal to come home. Peter Youngren

One day, Francis of Assisi was travelling along a narrow path when he saw a leper. Terrified of leprosy, he drew back, but then, feeling ashamed of his response, he ran and wrapped his arms about the leper's neck, kissed him, and passed on. Only moments later, he looked back, but the man had disappeared. From that day on, he was certain that it was not leper he had seen, but Christ Himself.

See if you can answer this question: Who is the greatest disciple of love in the New Testament? Did you think it was John because he talked about love so much? Wrong! Did you think it was Paul because he wrote the love chapter in 1 Corinthians 13? Wrong again! In fact it was Peter. After all, he asked Jesus to pray for his mother-in-law!

Love For God

A girl was with a group of teenagers at a party. "Let's go to a night club," someone suggested. "No, my parents wouldn't like that," she replied. One of the other girls said, "Afraid your father will hurt you?" "No," she replied. "I'm not afraid my father will hurt me. I'm afraid I might hurt him." That's the point, isn't it? I'm not afraid that my Father is going to punish me. I just don't want to do things that displease Him.

---

[54] D. Filkins, Kenneth *The Wittenburg Door*

Marriage

Husband to wife: "How do you expect me to remember your birthday when you never look any older?"

Husband: I'm the head of the home. My wife came to me on her knees. She said, "Get out from under there you coward!"

Does your wife pay you any compliments?" asked the curious bachelor. "Only in the winter," was the nonchalant reply. "Why in the winter?" "When the fire gets low she says, 'Alexander, the grate!'"

Husband and wife drove a long way in silence after a terrible argument in which neither would budge. He pointed to a mule in a paddock. "Relative of yours?" he asked. "Yes," she replied. "By marriage."

A man went to a counsellor for advice. His marriage was really bad and he wanted out, but he wanted to hurt his wife as much as possible. The counsellor thought for a while, then said, "I have an idea. This is the way to really hurt her. For the next three months, treat her like a princess. Love her, bring her flowers, buy her gifts, take her out to dinner, do some of the housework. Treat her like she's the most wonderful woman in the world. Then suddenly, you just leave. That'll really kill her." The man liked the advice. A few months later the counsellor saw him out walking and said, "So how's bachelor life treating you?" "What do you mean?" asked the man. "You know," said the counsellor. "How'd it go when you dumped your wife?" Looking perplexed, the man replied, "You've got to be kidding. I'm married to the most wonderful woman in the world." The counsellor walked away smiling to himself.

Technical Difficulties: Dear Tech Support, Last year I upgraded from Boyfriend 5.0 to Husband 1.0 and noticed that the new program began making unexpected changes to the accounting module, limiting access to flower and jewellery applications that had operated flawlessly under Boyfriend 5.0. In addition, Husband 1.0 uninstalled many other valuable programs, such as Romance 9.9 but installed undesirable programs such as NFL 5.0 and NBL 3.0. Furthermore, Conversation 8.0 no longer runs and Housecleaning 2.6 simply crashes the system. I've tried running Nagging 5.3 to fix these problems but to no avail – Desperate. Dear Desperate, Keep in mind, Boyfriend 5.0 is an entertainment package, while Husband 1.0 is an operating system. Try to enter the command: C:/ I THOUGHT YOU LOVED ME and install Tears 6.2. Husband 1.0 should then automatically run the applications: Guilty 3.0 and Flowers 7.0. But remember, overuse can cause Husband 1.0 to default to Grumpysilence 2.5, Happyhour 7.0 or Beer 6.1. Beer 6.1 is a very bad program that will create "Snoring Loudly" wave files. DO NOT install MotherInLaw 1.0 or reinstall another Boyfriend program. These are not supported applications and will crash Husband 1.0. In summary, Husband 1.0 is a great program, but it does have limited memory and cannot learn new applications quickly. Consider buying additional software to improve performance. I personally recommend Hot Food 3.0 and Lingerie 5.3 – Tech Support.

They've discovered something that will prevent AIDS – it's called a wedding ring.

A man went to a vet and asked him to cut off his dog's tail. Reluctant to perform the operation unless it was absolutely necessary, the vet asked about the reason. "Well," explained the owner, "my mother-in-law is coming for a visit and I don't want her to see any sign of a welcome."

Did you hear about the guy who went to the library and took out a book called *How to Hug*? He got home and found out it was volume seven of a set of encyclopaedias.

A derelict asked a man for ten dollars. The man said, "If I give you ten dollars, will you buy booze?" The derelict said no. The man asked, "Will you gamble with it?" Again the derelict said he wouldn't. "Then come home with me," the man said. "I want my wife to see what happens to a man who doesn't drink or gamble."

A woman was in the frozen-foods section of her local supermarket when she noticed a man shopping with his son. As she walked by, the man checked something off his list, and whispered conspiratorially to his child, "You know, if we really mess this up, we'll never have to do it again."

A man was nervously walking around the supermarket when he crashed into another man's trolley. "Watch where you're going!" snarled the other man. "I'm sorry!" said the first one, "I'm rather worried. I've been looking for my wife for fifteen minutes." "Me too! I'm looking for my wife too." "Why don't we look for them together, then?" "Great idea! What does your wife look like?" "She's blonde, blue-eyed, big luscious lips and she's wearing a tight, red dress with a plunging neckline. What does your wife look like?" "Forget my wife! Let's go and find yours!"

A couple had been married two years when the wife asked her husband for some money to buy a new dress. He demanded to know why she needed one. "Because," she replied, "I'm tired of people throwing confetti at me when I go shopping."

Scientists at Europe's annual Human Reproductive Conference advised that recent research revealed that beer contained female hormones. They recommended that men should carefully consider their beer consumption. The scientists' theory is that when men drink beer, they act like women. In an experiment, 100 men each consumed a six-pack of beer during a one hour period. Scientists observed that all of the men became very emotional, gained weight, talked a lot without making sense, argued over nothing, did not think rationally, were incapable of driving, had to sit while urinating, and would not apologise when wrong. No further testing was deemed necessary.

Marriages are made in heaven, but so are thunder and lightning. Marriage is when a man and woman become as one; the trouble is, who decides which one? Before marriage, a man yearns for the woman he loves; after marriage the "y" in "yearns" becomes silent. A man is incomplete until he marries; after that he's finished.

One man said, "I love being married. I was single for years, and I just got tired of finishing my own sentences."

A couple were getting ready for bed one night. "When I look in the mirror," said the wife, "all I see is an old woman. My face is wrinkled, and I'm flabby all over." Her husband was silent. "Hey!" she said, turning to him. "Can't you even say something positive to make me feel better about myself?" "Well," he said, "your eyesight is still perfect."

Everyone on earth dies and Peter tells all the men to form two lines. In one line are the men dominated by their wives, and in the other line are the men who dominated their wives. The line with the men dominated by their wives is hundreds of miles long. The other line has only one man in it. Peter is angry. He says, "All you men should be ashamed of yourselves allowing your wives to dominate you. Look at this man, the only one who stood up like a man. Tell me, my son, how did you do it?" "I don't know," said the man. "My wife told me to stand here."

A man said to his wife one day, "I don't know how you can be so stupid and so beautiful at the same time." The wife responded, "Allow me to explain. God made me beautiful so you would be attracted to me. God made me stupid so I would be attracted to you."

Men are always asking what women want in bed. The answer is breakfast. Kathy Lette

Marriage is a relationship in which one person is always right, and the other is a husband.

How To Make A Woman Happy: It's not difficult to make a woman happy. A man only needs to be: a friend; a companion; a lover; a brother; a father; a master; a chef; an electrician; a carpenter; a plumber; a mechanic; a decorator; a stylist; a sexologist; a gynaecologist; a psychologist; a pest exterminator; a psychiatrist; a healer; a good listener; an organizer; a good father; very clean; sympathetic; athletic; warm; attentive; gallant; intelligent; funny; creative; tender; strong; understanding; tolerant; prudent; ambitious; capable; courageous; determined; true; dependable; passionate; compassionate; as well as: give her compliments regularly; love shopping; be honest; be very rich; not stress her out; not look at other girls;

give her lots of attention, but expect little yourself; give her lots of time, especially time for herself; give her lots of space, never worry about where she goes; plus never to forget: birthdays, anniversaries, or arrangements she makes. How To Make A Man Happy: 1. Show up naked; 2. Bring food

Isn't it unfair that women love cats? Cats are independent, they don't listen, they don't come when you call, they like to stay out all night and when they are at home they like to be left alone to sleep. In other words, every quality that women hate in a man, they love in a cat. Terry Sangster

Shortly after getting married, a man stopped wearing his wedding ring. "Why don't you wear your wedding ring?" asked his wife. He replied, "Because it cuts off my circulation." "Well, that's what it's supposed to do," she said.

Of all my wife's relations, I like myself the best.

Most marriages break up for religious reasons. He thinks he's a god, and she doesn't.

Maturity

Maturity puts others first. You won't see a father pouting and saying about a baby, "It's not fair. He's getting fed before me."

Medical

In the first year of this voluntary … reporting system, 56 U.S. hospitals reported slightly more than 40,000 snafus. This year 500 hospitals came forward with 192,000 admissions of error. USP's database now lists more than 500,000 cases in which the wrong drug or wrong dose was prescribed (for example, a blood-pressure drug given to a patient who needed an antidepressant) or the proper treatment was administered the wrong way (say, by IV instead of feeding tube). The private nonprofit organisation expects its database to approach 1 million cases next year. The ultimate goal of the reporting system is to identify patterns of errors so they can be prevented. This year's report found that seniors suffer the most from hospitals' mistakes. Patients ages 65 and older accounted for more than a third of all medication errors and 55% of fatal errors.[55]

Thousands of Queenslanders are victims of hospital blunders every year, according to medical chiefs. Federal Government statistics show about 10,000 people die every year from medical errors. The Medical Error Action Group says the problem of hospital errors in Australia is "colossal". "There are cases where hospital staff are operating on the wrong limb, appendices have been removed instead of hernias, equipment is not being sterilised and hospitals are ignoring blood use-by dates," the lobby group's Lorraine Long said. ... But a black hole of medical error data in Queensland means the true number of mishaps is unknown, with admissions the system is flawed. Doctors and nurses are said to be reluctant to report mistakes for fear of reprisals. ... Chairman of the safety committee at Princess Alexandra Hospital Charles Mitchell said one of the most common sources of patient harm was medication mix-ups with nurses unable to read doctors' instructions.[56]

Doctors cannot determine the cause of 37% of physical symptoms reported by their patients.[57]

---

[55] *Time Magazine* December 1, 2003, David Bjerklie p75
[56] *Sunday Mail* 22-2-04 P33 (Reported by Jessica Lawrence)
[57] *Psychosomatics* as reported in *Reader's Digest* June 2004 p 95

18,000 people die each year from "adverse events" in our hospitals.[58]

Visiting a GP? There's an 83% chance you'll leave with a prescription, down from 94% in 1998.[59]

One medium-sized apple contains a third of your daily vitamin C needs.[60]

In the last five years, Britons have seen a 38% rise in repetitive strain injury of thumbs and wrists. The cause? Text messaging on mobile phones.[61]

Men

Ten men and one woman were hanging off a rope under a helicopter. Since the rope wasn't strong enough to carry them all, they decided someone had to leave. But they weren't able to decide who should go. Finally, with great emotion, the woman said that she would let go voluntarily as she had always given up everything for her husband, her sons, and men in general. Sacrificing for men had been her way of life. The men were so moved with her speech that as soon as she had finished, they all started clapping.

Asked by Spike TV to choose how they measure success, only 3% of men said through their work, while 31% said they did so through their faith in God, 26% through being the best person possible, 22% through their network of family and friends, and 17% through maintaining a balance between home and work.[62]

---

[58] *Reader's Digest* July 2005 p 73
[59] AIHW report as quoted in *Reader's Digest* April 2006 p30
[60] *Reader's Digest* May 2006 p 156
[61] *Reader's Digest* September 2006, p 16
[62] *Time* 23-8-04 p 41

Why do men respond to psychoanalysis more quickly than women? Because when the psychoanalyst wants them to go back to their childhood, they are already there.

Men are twice as likely as women to forget their partner's birthday.[63]

The chances of a family attending church if a child is converted is 3.5%. If the mother is converted, it's 17%. If the father is converted, it's 93%.

Mercy

I am not a naturally merciful person; I have a strong sense of justice. When I watch a movie, I want to see the bad guy get what's coming to him. The trouble is, when I stand before God, I don't want to receive what I deserve. What I want is mercy.

Mind

The greatest preacher you'll ever hear is yourself.

Victorious living is a struggle between the old man and the new man. It's like a dog-fight. If you feed one, it becomes strong and if you starve the other it becomes weak.

Everyone has a photographic memory; some just don't have film.

Carrying a photo of a loved one to reduce separation anxiety doesn't only work for humans. A new study has discovered sheep also experience separation anxiety – but looking at a photo of another sheep from the same breed will calm a stressed ewe. A team of scientists from Cambridge University found that when separated from their flock, the sheep stressed out,

[63] *Reader's Digest* May 2006 p 18

bleated and looked agitated. Their heart rate rose a whopping 20 beats per minute. When shown a photo of a familiar breed, their heart rate returned to normal. And wait for this: the response was even better if the sheep in the photo appeared normal and calm.[64]

In war, captors often try to mess with the minds of captives. One method is to give them a shovel, point to a huge pile of dirt, and tell them to move it to another point. Once that is done, they tell them to move it back. The idea is to remove their sense of purpose.

Numerous studies have shown that gentle exercise three times a week can improve concentration and abstract reasoning in older people, perhaps by stimulating the growth of new brain cells. Exercise also helps steady our blood glucose. As we age, our glucose regulation worsens, which causes spikes in blood sugar. This can affect the dentate gyrus, an area within the hippocampus that helps form memories.[65]

Ministry and Ministry Gifts

Pastor: "Say deacon, a mule died out in front of the church." Deacon: "Well it's the job of you ministers to look after the dead. Why tell me?" Pastor: "You're right; it is my job. But we always notify the next of kin."

The perfect minister: A computerised survey has indicated that the perfect minister preaches fifteen minutes, condemns sin but never upsets anyone, works from 8am till midnight, and is also a janitor. He makes $60 per week, wears good clothes, buys good

---

[64] *Reader's Digest* December 2004 p 12

[65] The Changing Brain *New Scientist Magazine* issue 2702

books, drives a good car and gives about $50 a week to the poor. He is 26 years old, but has been preaching 30 years. Wonderfully gentle and handsome, he has a burning desire to work with teenagers, and spends all his time with senior citizens. He smiles all the time with a straight face because he has a sense of humour that keeps him seriously dedicated to his work. He makes 15 calls daily on church families, shut-ins and the hospitalised. He spends all his time evangelising the unchurched and is always in his office when needed. If your minister does not measure up, simply send this letter to six other churches that are tired of their minister and send him to the church at the top of the list. In one week you will receive 1,643 ministers, and one of them should be perfect. Have faith in this letter. One church broke the chain and got its old minister back in less than three weeks.

Your trustworthiness may mean life to someone – your lack of integrity, *death*.[66]

Mission / Missions

Just to say I'm going to wherever, without the necessary planning, without the necessary training, is really a very ineffective way to do missions. Norm Bradshaw

A little girl at the beach had a box of chips. There were a few seagulls. The box had tipped over, but she was still eating the chips. Suddenly, the wind blew the box about four metres away and the little girl ran to get it. When she got back there wasn't a single chip left. The seagulls had had a feeding frenzy.

---

[66] Sandford, Paula *Healing Victims of Sexual Abuse* p75

Satan will always take advantage if we are distracted from the task.

Misunderstanding

Three sons were discussing the gifts they had bought their mother. The first had bought her a big house. The second had bought her a Mercedes with a driver. The third knew she loved the Bible so he said he'd bought her a parrot which had been specially trained to recite Bible verses. All she had to do was suggest a reference and the parrot would start reciting. The first son got a letter saying that it was a very nice house, but it was too big and took all her time to clean. The second son got a letter saying the car was much too big for her and besides, the driver was rude. The third son got a letter saying, "You're the only one who understands me. Your two brothers give me stuff I don't really want. But you're such a good son. Thank you. The chicken was delicious."

Money

A contemporary of Wesley's, named Fletcher, was informed by his patron that he could live in Durham in Cheshire. The patron said, "The parish is small, the duty is light, the income is good and it is situated in a fine healthy sporting country." "Alas, sir," answered Fletcher, "Durham will not suit me. There is too much money (£400 pa) and too little labour." The patron replied, "Few clergymen make such objections. It is a pity to decline such a living, as I do not know that I can find you another. Would you like Madeley?" "That sir would be the very place for me." "If you prefer Madeley, I shall find no difficulty in persuading the present vicar to exchange it for Durham, which is worth more than twice as much."

A boy swallowed a fifty cent coin and started to choke. His father frantically yelled for help. Meanwhile, a woman sitting outside a café drinking coffee heard the commotion, put down her magazine and cup, and sauntered over to the boy. She squeezed him powerfully till the coin popped out, caught it, handed it to the father and returned to her table. Amazed, and overcome with gratitude, the relieved father followed her. "That was awesome!" he said. "Are you a doctor?" "No," the woman replied. "I work for the taxation department."

Howard Hughes, manufacturer, aviator and motion picture producer, died in 1976 aged 70. In 1966 he sold his Trans World Airlines shares for over $500M. He was an enormously wealthy man. Yet he became deranged and emaciated from poor diet and excess drugs and died a recluse. Money didn't help him.

Warren Buffet is a living legend and one of the richest men in the world and he did it mainly from getting it right on the stockmarket. He started in 1956 with only $100. By 1969 he was sitting on top of $25 million. By 1993 his net worth was around $8 billion. And by 2000 the number crunchers said he was a $30 billion man – that's American dollars![67]

It was 1946 when Anne Scheiber invested $5,000 in the stock market. She put her share certificates away and left them there. By 1995, her investment had grown in value to $22 million!

690 million: Number of Asians living on $1 a day or less in 2002 – 223 million fewer than in 1990. 75%: Proportion of that decline occurring in China.[68]

---

[67] Switzer, Peter *Shares: Your Questions Answered* p82
[68] *Time Magazine* 20-9-04 p19

If more money and work will keep you out of church, the devil says, "I'll give it to you."

Queenslanders are wasting between $100-$150 a year leaving unused electrical appliances switched on at the wall. The worst offenders are desktop and laptop computers which can add $30 to your annual power bill if left on standby. A television digital converter box will cost you more than $25 extra a year, TVs range from $7 to $11 depending on size, VHS players $11, DVDs $15 and portable CD / radio boomboxes $6. The microwave – usually left on simply for the digital clock display – wastes $7. Even an electric toothbrush costs a couple of dollars when left on standby but not in use. ... Householders were notorious for switching television sets or stereos off at the remote, or putting the dishwashers and washing machines on as they walked out the door each morning. They all remained in the standby mode – using precious electricity.[69]

Money is better than poverty, if only for financial reasons. Woody Allen.

A couple living on a tight student budget, decided to pay off the hospital bill immediately after their child was born. One night, they were discussing how they could pay their other bills when the baby started crying for a nappy change. The mother picked him up, sighed, and said, "He's the only thing in the house that's paid for and he leaks!"

More money can be a trap, leading to more spending, more commitments, more worry, more complexity, more time on administering money, more desires, more time at work, less choice about how we spend

---

[69] *Sunday Mail* 2-1-05

our time, and degradation of our independence and life energy. Our lifestyle locks us into our "workstyle." Richard Koch

A rich person should leave his kids enough money to do something, but not enough to do nothing. Warren Buffett

We ruin our health to accumulate money, then we spend all our money to regain our health.

Research conducted by a leading compensation technology firm found that among employees planning to leave their companies, a majority felt they were underpaid. Fewer than 20 percent of them, however, were receiving less than the industry standard for their duties. Bill Coleman, of Salary.com, believes that many unhappy workers are overtitled rather than underpaid. Some companies give employees lofty titles even though their job responsibilities have not increased. In time, employees feel they deserve more money than their actual duties merit. "When it comes to salary," Coleman says, "it's what you do, not what you're called, that counts."[70]

Borrow money from pessimists; they don't expect it back.

Music

George Gershwin did not sit around waiting for inspiration to bring him good ideas. Oscar Levant, who lived with him, says Gershwin got more of his ideas just by playing. Whenever he sat down to the piano to amuse himself, something came of it. He looked upon his work as play. Creating his career was his way of having fun. His life was clear proof of

---

[70] *Our Daily Bread*, September 1, 2008

the theory that the way to learn how to do anything is to do it.

During a student orchestra rehearsal, the percussion section kept making mistakes. "When you're too dumb to play anything," the frustrated professor commented sarcastically, "they give you two sticks, place you at the back and call you a percussionist." One of the students whispered loudly, "And if you're too dumb to hold on to both sticks, they place you out front and call you a conductor."

Names

A couple of American non-believers steered clear of Biblical names for their new baby daughter. George and Tina Rollason, of York, Pennsylvania, have named her Atheist Evolution.[71]

What do these people have in common – Abram, Sarai, Jacob, Saul? They all had a change of name, to reflect a change of direction.

The Malaysian government is cracking down on ridiculous names. Some examples include: Ah Gong, which means Unsound Mind; Sum Seng, meaning Gangster; and Chow Tow, translated as Smelly Head.

Negativity

Some people are so negative, if you put them in a dark room, they'd develop.

If everything seems to be going well, you have obviously overlooked something.

New Covenant

The Old Covenant made provision for sin to be covered, whereas the New Covenant cleanses it. It's

---

[71] *Sunday Mail* Sept 1994

the same difference as covering a dirty shirt with a jacket or having it totally cleansed. God does not look at us through Christ so that His blood covers our sins. Rather, Christ's blood completely removes the stain of sin.

New Creation

A man went looking at real estate. The current owners realised that the property didn't look that good and assured him that they would do it up before he took possession. "Forget it," he said. "I don't want the building. I want the site." God isn't interested in our trying to fix up the building before we come to Him. He's interested in the site. Then He can build whatever He wants on it.

How To Flog A Dead Horse. The tribal wisdom of the Dakota Indians, passed on from generation to generation, says that when you discover that you are riding a dead horse, the best strategy is to dismount. Our modern bureaucrats, however, have a whole range of far more advanced strategies such as: Buying a stronger whip. Finding lighter riders. Harnessing several dead horses together to improve performance. Arranging an overseas visit to study dead horses. Reclassifying the horse as living impaired. Rewriting the performance requirements for dead horses. Providing additional funding to improve the performance of dead horses. Promoting the dead horse to a supervisory position. Any similarity between the above and what actually happens in government is purely intentional.[72] [A great example of why there's no use trying to fix up the Old Creation. Just let it stay dead.]

---

[72] *This 'n' That* p3

Obedience

If you deceive somebody else you are wicked but smart; if you deceive yourself you are wicked but stupid. Juan Carlos Ortiz on James 1:22 (hearing and not doing)

A ton of prayer will never produce what an ounce of obedience will. After all the praying, if you don't obey, you nullify all the praying.[73]

Obedience is like a computer password to the riches of God.

When they put up a skyscraper, they put a lot of work into the foundation before they start worrying about the walls. They'll want to make sure it will keep standing. Obedience to God is the best foundation to lay when building our lives.

Occult

49% of [Australian] women have sought the advice of a psychic or astrologer. 84% of women believe houses can be haunted.[74]

Why do psychics have to ask you for your name?

Timed births are becoming popular with couples in central India. Parents-to-be are increasingly opting to have their children delivered at the time suggested to them by local astrologers. The right timing of an "astro-child" is said to be a surefire way to ensure its health, happiness and success, reports *The Telegraph* of Calcutta. Dr Kiran Julkar, who runs a Bhopal nursing home, says, "If parents insist on some auspicious time, we oblige them depending on the health of the baby and the would-be mother."

---

[73] Cole, Edwin Louis *Maximised Manhood* p105
[74] *Reader's Digest* March 2004 p32-33

Astrologer Swami Trilokinathji Maharaj says: "Financial aptitude, fame and fortune, career – everything could be ensured by timing the birth."[75]

I almost had a psychic girlfriend, but she left me before we met.

Opportunity

If opportunity doesn't knock, build a door. Milton Berle, comedian

Early 20th century London newspaper ad by famous South Pole explorer Sir Ernest Shackleton: "Men wanted for hazardous journey. Small wages, bitter cold, long months of complete darkness, constant danger. Safe return doubtful." The response was so overwhelming that Shackleton wrote later, "It seemed as though all the men in Great Britain were determined to accompany us." How many have the courage, and are just waiting for the opportunity and a leader with a vision?

Opposition

In the same sense that a secret agent sends out a signal that merits serious attention by the opposition, so the Christian walking in obedience to the Spirit of God, abiding in prayer, and committed to the kingdom stirs enemy opposition. The stakes are higher for the veteran who can do the most damage to the domain of darkness. My premise should be clear by now: any servant of Jesus Christ who poses a serious threat to the powers of hell will be targeted and will encounter resistance, especially at times of strategic ministry.[76]

---

[75] *Reader's Digest* March 2005 p 13
[76] Thomas B. White (*The Believer's Guide to Spiritual Warfare*) as quoted in C. Peter Wagner *Territorial Spirits* p65-66

Pain

Pain is like an alarm. Sometimes you get huge amounts of pain for relatively minor things. If somebody bends your fingernail back, it's torture. Your body is saying, "Take care of this. I don't care if you didn't finish your sandwich." If you don't have pain, you'll think, maybe I'll finish my sandwich. That's not good for survival.[77]

Parents

The Housewife's Lament
I'm just a little housewife,
With dishes three times a day.
With laundry and cleaning and cooking,
And toys to put away.
Now, it's not that I mind the housework,
Or the screaming kids at play.
It's that husband who burns me up when he says,
"Did you do anything today?" Anon.

"The US FDA has approved the first-ever transdermal patch for the treatment of depression," Tina Fey announced on *Saturday Night Live*. "Simply remove the backing and press the patch firmly over your mother's mouth."[78]

In Chile, a 65-year-old woman (Leonita Albina) has had 55 documented births; she claims to have had 64 children.

Motherhood is not for the fainthearted. Used frogs, skinned knees, and the insults of teenage girls are not meant for the wimpy. Danielle Steel

---

[77] Interview with leading surgeon Kenneth Kamler (expert on the body's ability to adapt to hostile environments) as reported in *Reader's Digest* December 2004 p 50

[78] *Reader's Digest* January 2007 p 25

Attendance Study: A study once disclosed that if both Mom and Dad attend church regularly, 72 percent of their children remain faithful in attendance. If only Dad attends regularly, 55 percent remain faithful. If only Mom attends regularly, 15 percent remain faithful. If neither attend regularly, only 6 percent remain faithful. Warren Muller.

Patience

An old train was crawling slowly through the countryside when it suddenly came to a complete stop. The solitary traveller in the carriage, a salesman, asked the conductor why they had stopped. The conductor said, "Nothing to be concerned about, sir. There's a cow on the tracks." About ten minutes later, the train started off again, but after creeping along for only another couple of kilometres, it ground to a halt again. "This is just a brief delay," said the conductor. "We'll get going again soon." The frustrated salesman asked, "What is it this time? Did we catch up to the cow again?"

The most important thing that ever happened to this planet was the coming of Jesus. You'd think that God would be in a real hurry. But Jesus was a full-term baby. Conception, development, birth, growth, all in the usual time-frames.

Peace

You can purchase sleep from the chemist but you can't purchase rest.

Nicholas Ridley (1500 – 1555) had been condemned to death for his faith. The night before, his brother offered to stay with him in prison. Ridley said that he planned to sleep as well as usual. The next day he encouraged another Christian who was being executed. "Be of good heart, brother, for God will either assuage the fury of the flame, or else strengthen us to abide it." They knelt and prayed next to the stake, talked briefly, then were burned.

Peer Pressure

If you've never laid your head under a semi-trailer, how do you know you won't like it till you try it? Sound dumb? This is the same argument used to get someone to try drugs.

Perception

It's All So Ovibuos: Aoccdrnig to rscheearch at an Elingsh uinervtisy, it deosn't mttaer in waht oredr the ltteers in a wrod are, the olny iprmoetnt tihng is taht frist and lsat ltteer is at the rghit pclae. The rset can be a toatl mses and you can sitll raed it wouthit porbelm. Tihs is bcuseae we do not raed ervey lteter by istlef but the wrod as a wlohe.[79]

Persecution

Do people treat you like dirt? God took a lump of dirt and transformed it into a man.

Pliny the Younger (A.D. 62-113) to emperor Trajan: The method I have observed towards those who have been denounced as Christians is this: I interrogated them whether they are Christians; if they confessed it I repeated the question twice again, adding the threat of capital punishment; if they still persevered, I ordered them to be executed ... Those who denied they were or had ever been, Christians, who repeated after me an invocation to the gods, and who offered adoration, with wine and frankincense, to your image

---

[79] Johnathan Powell as quoted in *Reader's Digest* November 2004 p 146

... and who finally cursed Christ – none of which acts, it is said, those who are really Christians can be forced into performing – these I thought it proper to discharge ...

Nero lit his gardens by wrapping Christians in pitch and setting them alight. He sewed others into animal skins and set his dogs on them to tear them apart. Others were tortured on the rack or scraped with pincers. Molten lead was poured on them, their eyes were torn out, red hot brass plates fixed to the most sensitive parts of their bodies, parts of their bodies cut off and roasted in front of them, hands and feet burned while cold water was poured on them to prolong the pain. [80]

Su Kim's teacher promised her a special prize. "After your parents go to bed tonight, if you can find a black book at home, bring it to school tomorrow. But don't tell anyone." She was excited about the possibility of winning a prize, and looked diligently. Su Kim found a book – a Bible – and the next day took it to her teacher. But when she returned home from school, her parents were gone. They'd been arrested by the North Korean police. Their crime was owning a Bible. After a frightening night home alone, Su Kim became a state orphan.

Perseverance

John wanted to be a writer. He wrote his first book and submitted it to a publisher. Sometime later he received a rejection slip. He tried again. He got another rejection slip. He tried again and got another. 100, 200 – most people would have given up. He received more than 700 rejection slips until finally his

---

[80] Source: Barclay, William *Daily Study Bible: Vol 1 – Matt 1-10* p 112

first book was published in 1932. John Creasey went on to write over 600 books under 17 pseudonyms and founded the Crime Writers' Association in 1953.

Fred Astaire was one of the top singers, dancers and actors of all time. In *Top Hat*, *Swing Time*, *Holiday Inn*, and other famous movies, he proved himself to be the consummate entertainer. But when he was starting out in 1932, a Hollywood talent judge wrote on his screen test: "Can't act. Can't sing. Can dance a little."

From John Wesley's diary: Sunday morning, May 5, preached in St. Ann's, was asked not to come back anymore. Sunday p.m., May 5, preached at St. John's, deacons said, "Get out and stay out." Sunday a.m., May 12, preached at St. Jude's, can't go back there either. Sunday p.m., May 12, preached at St. George's, kicked out again. Sunday a.m., May 19, preached at St. somebody else's, deacons called a special meeting and said I couldn't return. Sunday p.m., May 19, preached on the street, kicked off the street. Sunday a.m., May 26, preached in meadow, chased out of meadow as a bull was turned loose during the services. Sunday a.m., June 2, preached out at the edge of town, kicked off the highway. Sunday p.m., June 2, afternoon service, preached in a pasture, 10,000 people came to hear me.[81]

In 1947, Lester Wunderman was arbitrarily fired from his advertising job in New York. But he felt he still had a lot to learn from the head of the agency, Max Sackheim. So the next morning Wunderman went back to his office and began working as he had before. He talked to co-workers and clients; he sat in on meetings – all without pay. Sackheim ignored him

---

[81] Newman, Bill *The Ten Laws Of Leadership* p40-41

for a month. Finally he walked up to Wunderman: "Okay, you win," he said, shaking his head. "I never saw a man who wanted a job more than he wanted money." Wunderman went on to be one of the most successful advertising men of the century. He's credited with having invented preprinted newspaper inserts, plus subscription cards such as those used by Time-Life Books and the Columbia Record Club; ideas that have produced billions of dollars in profit.[82]

Personality

A Type A personality is thought to be made up of three parts: competitiveness, hostility and time urgency/impatience, or TUI. Research in the past has shown that competitiveness is not linked to health problems, whereas hostility is. Now a pioneering study has implicated TUI too. Lead author Li Jing Yan of Northwestern University enlisted more than 3,000 young adults – men and women, black and white – between 18 and 30 and tracked them for 15 years. She asked them to consider four traits: 1) a tendency to get upset when having to wait, 2) a tendency to eat too quickly, 3) a feeling of pressure as the end of the regular workday approaches and 4) a feeling of time pressure in general. The respondents were then asked to rate how well these traits described them, on a scale from "very well" to "not at all." By year 13, a clear trend had emerged. Those who gave positive responses to all areas were twice as likely as the others to have developed moderate to severe hypertension (blood pressure of 140/90 or higher). ... uncontrolled hypertension could lead to

---

[82] Rhema Broadcasting Group

heart disease, stroke, kidney failure and even dementia.[83]

Perspective (see also Faith Perspective)

My Christian brothers went on to make another startling statement. "Khomeini has been the biggest blessing our country has ever had," they told me, "because he has revealed Islam for what it really is. Before he came, Islam was a pretty package all wrapped up on the mantelpiece. Khomeini took the parcel, undid the wrapping, and showed the world what is really inside."[84]

Do infants enjoy infancy as much as adults enjoy adultery? How is it possible to have a civil war? If one synchronised swimmer drowns, do the rest drown too? It you eat pasta and antipasto, would you still be hungry? If you try to fail, and succeed, which have you done? Why is it called tourist season if we can't shoot at them? Before they invented drawing boards, what did they go back to? If all the world is a stage, where is the audience sitting? If love is blind, why is lingerie so popular? If the #2 pencil is the most popular, why is it still #2? If work is so terrific, how come they have to pay you to do it? If you're born again, do you have two bellybuttons? How do I set my laser printer on stun?

Why did the chicken cross the road? Kindergarten Teacher: To get to the other side. Aristotle: For the greater good. Karl Marx: It was a historical inevitability. Saddam Hussein: This was an unprovoked act of rebellion and we were quite justified in dropping fifty tons of nerve gas on it.

---

[83] Sanjay Gupta, M.D. (neurosurgeon and a CNN medical correspondent) in *Time Magazine* 2-12-02 p127

[84] Brother Andrew *The Muslim Challenge* p6

Captain James T. Kirk: To boldly go where no chicken has gone before. Hippocrates: Because of an excess of phlegm in its pancreas. Martin Luther King, Jr.: I envision a world where all chickens will be free to cross roads without having their motives called into question. Fox Mulder: You saw it cross the road with your own eyes. How many more chickens have to cross the road before you believe it? Freud: The fact that you are at all concerned that the chicken crossed the road reveals your underlying sexual insecurity. Einstein: Whether the chicken crossed the road or the road moved beneath the chicken depends upon your frame of reference. Colonel Sanders: I missed one!

I used to eat a lot of natural foods until I learned that most people die of natural causes.

When weeding, the best way to make sure you are removing a weed and not a valuable plant is to pull on it; if it comes out of the ground easily, it's a valuable plant.

Tom, Jack and George all signed up to join the police force. They were being trained by a detective who had a photo of a man. He showed it to Tom for five seconds and said, "Take a good look." Then he took it away and said, "What did you notice about this man? How would you describe the suspect?" "That's easy," replied Tom. "He only has one eye." "Don't be silly. It only looks as if he has one eye because it's a profile." He showed the photo to Jack. "What did you notice about this man? How would you describe the suspect?" "That's easy," replied Jack. "He only has one ear." "Don't be silly. It only looks as if he has one ear because it's a profile." He showed the photo to George. "Now think before you say anything silly. What did you notice about this man? How would you describe the suspect?" "That's easy," replied George.

"He's wearing contact lenses." The detective looked puzzled. "Just a moment," he said, and walked out of the room. He checked the man's file, and found that he did wear contact lenses. Returning to the room, he said, "That's amazing. How on earth did you do that?" "It was easy," replied George. "He couldn't possibly be wearing glasses, because he's only got one eye and one ear."

Bear in mind: the thoughts of unhappy, anxious and depressed people contain gross distortions. Unhappy people tell themselves lies and untruths about their lives, their opportunities and setbacks, their friends and family, their luck and mistakes, then formulate a barely conscious philosophy that, since it does not conform to reality, causes them more unhappiness. It's as if they look at the world through a dark prism that distorts their view of reality.[85]

One in two parents of obese children believe their child is "normal weight" or "underweight".[86]

Tom Watson, Sr., for over forty years the founder and leader of IBM, was a firm believer that failures are learning experiences. One time, when an upcoming junior executive lost over $10 million on a risky venture, Watson called him into his office. Nervously, the junior executive asked, "I guess you want my resignation?" Watson was surprised. He said, "You can't be serious. We've just spent $10 million educating you!"

The Pecking Order: When I take a long time, I am slow, but when my Boss takes a long time, he is thorough. When I don't do a task, I am lazy, but when my boss doesn't do it, he is too busy. When I do

---

[85] *Reader's Digest* July 2005 p 81

[86] *Reader's Digest* October 2005 p 18

something without being told, I am over-stepping my boundaries, but when my boss does the same thing, that's initiative. When I take a stand, I am stubborn, but when my boss does it, he is being firm. When I overlook a rule of etiquette, I am rude, but when my boss breaks a few rules, he is being original. When I please my boss, I am apple polishing, but when my boss pleases his boss, he is cooperating. When I get ahead, I am lucky, but when my boss gets ahead, that's hard work.[87]

Plans

When D L Moody, great American evangelist of the last century, lay on his deathbed, he was reputed to have said to his sons, "If God be your partner, make your plans large."

Most people are better at planning their next vacation than they are at planning their own personal growth.

Pleasing God

The triumph of Jesus Christ at the very juncture over the powers and principalities of evil is a major theme of the New Testament. He was tested by persecution at his birth and throughout his life. He was tested by false friends, by hostile religious leaders, by Jewish and Gentile civil authorities. He was tested in the healings, the exorcisms, the temptations in the wilderness. The principalities and powers attacked him through opposition from within his own circle. His own family assigned his notoriety to the devil (Mk 3:20-35) and one of his intimate friends sold him for thirty pieces of silver. No man was ever tested like Jesus Christ. He faced it all, and overcame it all, as no man before or since has done. The secret of his

---

[87] *North Lakes Messenger* 16th July, 2007. p 29

life was his determination to please his heavenly Father at all points. (John 8:29)[88]

Pleasing People

The spirit of Saul: I gave the people what they wanted. Mark T. Barclay

Politics & Politicians

What do you call ten politicians at the bottom of the Suez Canal? A start.

Employment ad for dead politicians: Wanted, blokes to rule heaven, must be able to vote own pay rises, call each other names, and pass useless laws. No experience necessary.

Popularity

If you don't want any criticism, all you have to do is say nothing, do nothing, and be nothing. Duane Vanderklerk

What is popular is not always right; what is right is not always popular.

Pornography

As of July 2003, there were 260 million pages of pornography online, an increase of 1800% since 1998. Porn amounts to about 7% of the 3.3 billion Web pages indexed by Google. Internet users who access adult websites spend an average of 73 minutes per month there, but that doesn't include time spent on amateur porn sites. Americans rent upwards of 800 million pornographic videos and DVDs a year, compared with 3.6 billion nonpornographic videos. Nearly 1 in 5 rentals is a

---

[88] Michael Green (*I Believe In Satan's Downfall*) as quoted in C. Peter Wagner *Territorial Spirits* p186

porn flick. Hollywood produces 400 feature films a year. The porn industry churns out 11,000. One in 4 American adults surveyed in 2002 admitted to seeing an X-rated movie in the past year.[89]

Possessions

The Christians, you know, worship a man to this day – the distinguished personage who introduced their novel rites, and was crucified on that account... You see, these misguided creatures start with the general conviction that they are immortal for all time, which explains the contempt of death and voluntary self-devotion which are so common among them; and then it was impressed on them by their original lawgiver that they are all brothers, from the moment that they are converted, and deny the gods of Greece, and worship the crucified sage, and live after his laws. All this they take quite on faith, with the result that they despise all worldly goods alike, regarding them merely as common property. Lucian (2nd century Greek satirist):

Power

Pope Gregory was showing Thomas Aquinas all the treasures of the Vatican. The Pope said, "We can no longer say with Peter, silver and gold have I none." "Yes," replied Aquinas. "But no longer can we say in the name of Jesus Christ of Nazareth rise up and walk."

The greatest force in the world? Compound interest. Albert Einstein

James Brown, credited with inventing soul, funk, and hip-hop was performing in Boston the night Martin Luther King was murdered. He managed to control

---

[89] *Time Magazine* 19th January, 2004, p75

the crowd. Responding to a comment on the power he was wielding to be able to do that, Brown said, "That's not power. That's influence. Only God has power."

Law of Deadly Force: Use the least amount of power to deal with a situation. Too much is the wrong application of force; for example, shooting someone for jay walking.

A logging foreman sold a farmer a chainsaw. He said, "This is guaranteed to chop down fifty trees a day." The farmer was impressed with that. A week later, the farmer stormed back through the front door, threw the saw on the counter, and demanded his money back. "There's something wrong with this saw. There's no way it'll do fifty trees a day. It can hardly do three trees a day!" The foreman grabbed the saw, pulled the cord, and the saw went, "Bzzzzzzz." The farmer jumped back, eyes wide open: "Hey, what's that noise?" For so many Christians, God's power is available to them, but they simply don't know how to access it.

David Brainard, missionary to the Susquehanna, Delaware and Stockbridge Indians once preached through an intoxicated interpreter who was so drunk he could barely stand. Yet scores were converted through the preaching. Brainard's secret was his prayerfulness.

Praising God

Once upon a time there was a king who went hunting game with his friend. As the king shot the arrow, his thumb came off. His friend said, "Praise God because He's in control." The king was furious and threw his friend in gaol. Sometime later, the king was hunting when he ventured into a distant land where

165

he'd never been before. Suddenly he was surrounded by cannibals. They tied him up and were ready to cook him when they saw the hand with no thumb. "No perfect, no cookie," said the chief, and they let him go. He went back to his friend and apologised. "You were right. Not having a thumb saved my life." His friend said, "Praise God that I have been in gaol for so long." "How can you praise God?" the king asked. His friend replied, "If I hadn't been in gaol, I would have been hunting with you. And look: two thumbs."

Faith is giving glory to God when you're in the valley; anyone can do it on the peak.

When you use a magnifying glass, it doesn't change the size of what you look at. It changes your perception. Dwayne Vanderklok, on magnifying the Lord.

Prayer

A Suggested Daily Prayer: Lord, so far today, I am doing all right. I have not gossiped, lost my temper, been greedy, grumpy, nasty, selfish or self-indulgent. I have not whined, cursed or eaten any chocolate. However, I am going to get out of bed in a few minutes and I will need a lot more help after that.

A woman was driving along when she saw a tornado coming her way, so she pulled over, and moments later watched as a house was demolished. Once the tornado had passed, she rushed over and saw a man coming out of a hole in the ground. "Are you okay?" she asked. "Is there anyone else in there?" "Nope," said the man. "Just me and God having an urgent conversation."

Pray for your pastors; the tree at the top of the hill feels the wind the strongest.

The Difference
I got up early one morning
And rushed right into the day;
I had so much to accomplish
That I didn't have time to pray.

Problems just tumbled about me,
And heavier came each task.
"Why doesn't God help me?" I wondered.
He answered, "You didn't ask."

I wanted to see joy and beauty,
But the day toiled on, grey and bleak;
I wondered why God didn't show me.
He said, "But you didn't seek."

I tried to come into God's presence;
I used all my keys at the lock.
God gently and lovingly chided,
"My child, you didn't knock."

I woke up early this morning,
And paused before entering the day;
I had so much to accomplish
That I had to take time to pray. Author unknown

Corrie Ten Boom, a woman famous for her accounts of how God brought her through while in a German concentration camp in World War 2, author of numerous books, once told the story of how she was hospitalised with a fracture. There she was with numerous speaking engagements, and stuck in a hospital bed. When she prayed, God spoke to her along these lines, "Corrie, you've been so busy lately, you don't spend time with Me like you used to. I've missed you."

If you are connected to the internet, you know that there are basically two kinds of connection – dial-up and broadband. The major difference is this: broadband is connected all the time. I want to ask you a question: Do you have dial-up Christianity, or are you a broadband Christian? I'm a broadband Christian; I'm connected all the time. And the reason for that is that I have Jesus living within me. I don't need dial-up Christianity; I don't need to go to a priest to worship, or to a particular building, or to the virgin Mary, or anyone else. I am connected directly to God, through Christ, all the time.

Selfish praying: Several centuries ago, John Ward, a member of British Parliament prayed, "O Lord, You know that I have nine houses in the city of London, and that I have lately purchased an estate in Essex. I beseech You to preserve the two counties of Middlesex and Essex from fire and earthquakes. And as I have also a mortgage in Hertfordshire, I beg You also to have an eye of compassion on that county, and for the rest of the counties, You may deal with them as You may. O Lord, enable the banks to answer all their bills, and make all the debtors good men. Give prosperous voyage and safe return to the *Mermaid Sloop*, because I have not insured it. And because You have said, 'The days of the wicked are but short,' I trust You that You will not forget Your promise, as I have an estate that I will inherit on the death of that poor profligate young man, Sir J. L. Preserve me from thieves and housebreakers, and make all my servants so honest and faithful that they may always attend to my interests, and never cheat me out of my property night or day."

Before the Battle of Trafalgar, Nelson went to his cabin and knelt at the table, and wrote this prayer:

"May the Great God, whom I worship, grant to my country, and for the benefit of Europe in general, a great and glorious victory; and may no misconduct in any one tarnish it; and may humanity after victory be the predominant feature in the British Fleet. For myself, individually, I commit my life to Him who made me, and may His blessing light upon my endeavours for serving my country faithfully. To Him I resign myself and the just cause which is entrusted to me to defend. Amen, Amen, Amen."

Preaching

A man commented to a preacher that preaching was a waste of time because most sermons were soon forgotten. "That may be," replied the preacher. "But my wife has cooked me about 3,650 meals over the past ten years. I can't remember what they were, but I sure am well-fed."

God put a secret agent inside of you; his name is conscience. Peter Youngren on the conscience functioning to confirm the preaching of God's Word.

The man who shoots above the target does not prove thereby that he has superior ammunition. He just proves that he cannot shoot. James Denney, Scottish preacher, on keeping the gospel simple.

Heart of a preacher: Back in John Wesley's time, laymen were encouraged to preach sermons even though they were not well educated. Using Luke 19:21 – I feared You, because You are an austere man – as his text, and not understanding the meaning of the word "austere," one man thought the Scripture was talking about "an oyster man." He carefully explained how an oyster diver would cut his hands on the jagged shells as he groped in the cold, dark water to retrieve oysters. He talked about how he would then return to the surface holding the oyster "in his torn and bleeding hands." He then explained how Jesus came from heaven to this sinful world "in order to retrieve humans and bring them back up with Him to the glory of heaven. His torn and bleeding hands are a sign of the value He has placed on the object of His quest." At the end of the sermon, twelve men gave their lives to Christ. Later that evening a man approached Wesley grumbling about uneducated preachers who did not understand the Scriptures they were preaching about. Wesley, educated at Oxford University replied, "Never mind. The Lord got a dozen oysters tonight."

A pastor had preached for a long time, boring everyone silly. At the end of the message, everyone filed out of the meeting quietly without making eye contact with the preacher. Finally, an old man stopped and said to him, "Thank you, pastor. That message reminded me of the peace of God and love of God." Delighted, the pastor asked, "How did it remind you of God's peace and love?" "Oh," said the old man. "It reminded me of the peace of God because it passed all understanding, and the love of God because it went on and on forever."

Predestination

A group of theologians was divided into two factions. A little confused, one person approached the Calvinists. "Who sent you?" they asked. "Nobody. I came of my own free will." "Well you can't come here," they replied. So he went to the Arminian group. "Why did you choose our group?" they asked. "I didn't. They sent me," he answered, pointing to the Calvinists. "Well you can't stay here," was the reply.

Preparation

Jesus was a full term baby; God didn't hurry the process. Trevor Chandler

No matter what happens, the US Navy is not going to be caught napping. Frank Knox, Secretary of the US Navy, three days before the Japanese attack on Pearl Harbour.

Pride [See Also Humility]

"Change your course five degrees south to avoid collision," said the Captain. "Change your course five degrees north to avoid collision," came the reply. "This is the Captain speaking. I said to change your course five degrees south." "This is the First Seaman speaking. Change your course five degrees north." "Change your course five degrees south. This is the Captain of a destroyer." "Change your course five degrees north. This is a lighthouse."

Australia has long debated whether to become a republic. But for many of us, merely ditching the British monarchy isn't enough. The country is now thought to have around 20 "sovereign nations" and numbers are rising. Mainly founded by eccentrics wanting to break away from the strictures of central government, the states include the Hutt River Province in Western Australia, ruled by Prince Leonard and Princess Shirley; the Empire of Atlantium, based in the one-bedroom Sydney flat of George Cruickshank; and the Gay and Lesbian Kingdom of the Coral Sea – an archipelago of islands situated off the coast of Queensland, ruled by His Majesty Emperor Dale. Many of these microscopic states were formed for as trivial a reason as a would-be monarch getting annoyed at the local council for refusing permission to build a new front drive. It will come as little surprise that, according to constitutional lawyer Professor George Williams of the University of New South Wales, they have no legal status whatsoever.[90]

A young girl went to her pastor and confessed that she feared she had committed the sin of vanity. "What makes you think that?" asked the minister. "Because every morning when I look into the mirror I think how beautiful I am." "Never fear, my girl," was the reassuring reply. "That isn't a sin, it's only a mistake."

A car skidded on a wet road and hit a telegraph pole. A number of bystanders saw the accident and ran over to help. The first to reach the crash victim was a woman, but a man raced in, pushed her out of the way, and said, "Outta the way lady. I've taken a course in first-aid." The woman watched for a little while, then said, "Excuse me, but when you get to the part about calling a doctor, I'm right here."

Priorities

Jesus was often busy, but He was never in a hurry. You never see Him saying irritably, "Who touched my coat? I've gotta be at the mountain to preach in five minutes!"

Problems

When is a bird bigger than a house? When it's closer than the house. It's not really bigger. It just looks that way because it's closer. Problems can be like that. They can look much bigger than God if they are closer.

---

[90] *Reader's Digest* September 2005 p 97

Procrastination

The devil's favourite word is not a cuss word. The devil's favourite word is "tomorrow". James deMelo

When is the best time to plant a tree? Ten years ago. When is the second best time? Today.

Promises

We were walking round a shopping centre in Melaka, Malaysia, when we were offered a glass of green liquid to drink. I was the only one game enough to try it. It didn't have much flavour, and it turned out to be liquid chlorophyll being marketed by Excellent Healthy Enterprise in Melaka. The brochure they handed us listed "some of the possible remedial effects of liquid chlorophyll" as follows: "cleanse up body thoroughly, stop bacterial growth, improve oral health and hygiene, increase the blood count in anaemia, detoxifying the liver, solve arthritic and rheumatic problems, cure for diabetic, cure for stomach ulcers, regulating monthly menstruation punctual, decrease acidity in the body, maintain smooth healthy bloodstream, improve our appetite, reduce fatigue, improve insomnia, reduce constipation, good for cystitis or inflammation of the bladder, good for the heart."

Breaking a promise is like fishing. You cast your hook out with a worm on it, reel it in, and the fish never actually gets the worm. (At least it isn't supposed to. They always seem to get mine!)

Prophecy

If five percent of the prophecies I had heard over the years had been true, we would already have taken the world for Jesus. Wynne Lewis

Prosperity

If increase in money and work keeps you out of church, the devil says, "I'll give it to you."

The biggest problem with the Laodiceans was their *bragging* about their prosperity, not their prosperity. Mark T. Barclay

Provision

A Russian immigrant bought a ticket on a ship to the USA. So that he wouldn't get hungry, his mother gave him a loaf of black bread, which he divided up to last the trip. Each day, he'd look into the dining room and see all the people banqueting. It wasn't till the end of the trip that he discovered the fare included the food.

Pruning

The fruit tree is never so close to the gardener as when he has the knife in his hands.

Punctuality

A nationwide synchronisation of watches marked the start of a campaign to stamp out the country's legendary tardiness. Locals run on what is referred to as "Ecuadorian time," meaning most people turn up for appointments at least 15 minutes late. The civic group behind the scheme puts the cost of this lax approach at more than $700 million a year. The campaign has the backing of President Lucio Gutierrez .. who is often as much as three hours late for meetings.[91]

---

[91] *Time Magazine*, October 13, 2003, p 21

Punishment

The various enactments originating from the Black Act of 1732 were framed so broadly that the death penalty could be imposed for innumerable unspecified variations of the same offence, and it is impossible to compute precisely how many crimes there were which could be punished by death. Some say more than three hundred. Popularly known as the Bloody code, this legislation made it an offence punishable by death for a man, woman or child to steal turnips, shoot rabbit, pick a pocket, damage a fish-pond, cut down an ornamental tree, set fire to a haystack, consort with gypsies, write a threatening letter, impersonate a pensioner of Greenwich Hospital, or appear on a public highway with a sooty face. Such crimes were punished with a barbarism unparalleled in the history not only of England but of the whole civilised world. The records of children hanged during this period are numerous.[92]

Purity

A 17-year-old girl pressured by her friends to sleep with her boyfriend said, "I can be like you any time I choose, but you can never be like me."

Purpose

At a church camp, the speaker was talking about how God has a purpose for everything in His creation. He explained that there were reasons for dirt, wind, trees, animals, even cockroaches. One of the children raised his hand to ask a question: "If everything God made has a purpose, why did He make poison ivy?" That really stumped the speaker, till one of the children made a suggestion: "God made poison ivy

---

[92] Bailey, Brian *Hangman* pp 44,45

because He wanted us to know that there are some things we should keep our grubby little hands off."

Pulling into the campsite, three children jumped from the camper van and frantically began unloading equipment and setting up the tent. Mother and daughter set up the stove, while the boys ran around gathering firewood. Watching on, a nearby camper remarked, "That is amazing. How did you train your family to work like a team?" The father responded, "Oh, that's easy. No one is allowed to go to the bathroom till everything is set up."

Reading

According to Professor Henry Mayer who did an analytical survey of Australian newspapers, they comprised the following: Advertising – 58.6%; Foreign news – 7.4%; Political, social and economic news – 8.2%; Sport – 15%; Other news – 10.8%; Total news = 41.4%.[93]

Reconciliation

When you see someone driving towards you on your side of the road, and they're drunk, doing 130kmh, and swerving all over the place, you don't just think, "Well, I'm sober and doing the speed limit. I'm in the right, let them move." Paul Newsham

Redemption

If you put a couple of dollars in a Coke machine and get a Fanta, you don't care about the thing you got, you're more interested in the fact that you didn't get what you paid for. Is Jesus Christ getting what He paid for?

---

[93] Garvin, Mal *Us Aussies* by, quoting from Mayer, Henry *The Press In Australia*

Back in the days of the Roman Empire, a slave might go to the temple treasury and pay money into the treasury to buy his freedom. Technically, he was being purchased by some god or other and might have some religious obligations, but in reality he was now free. With the Jews it was a little different: Let's just say that I'm the owner of an ox a few thousand years ago and my ox gores someone so that he dies. The first time it happens I'd be okay. I wouldn't be held accountable for what my ox had done. But if I had already been warned once about the ox's tendency to have a go at people, not only would the ox be stoned but so would I. There was only one way out: I might be allowed to pay for my life. (Exodus 21:28-30) That act of buying back my forfeited life, or of the slave buying his freedom was called redemption.

Regret

One of the most useful functions that a computer can perform is editing. Using this feature, you can cut out things you don't want in a document and put them somewhere else, or get rid of them altogether. Sometimes it would be nice if life had an edit function.

Rejection

When you have a fear of rejection, you allow others to mold you into their expectations and desires. Wayne Cordeiro

Relationship/s

Desperate and lonely for female company, a frog telephoned a psychic telephone service to find out what his future held. The person on the other end of the line said, "You will meet a beautiful young woman who will find you very interesting and want to know all about you." Excited and amazed, the frog asked excitedly, "That's wonderful! Where will I meet her? At work? At a party?" "No," said the psychic. "In a biology class."

Remembering

Bill Cosby said that the remedy for forgetting what it was you went into that other room to get was to whack yourself on the bottom. He said that as soon as you return to the other room and sit down, that's when you remember, so it must be the pressure on the behind that helps.

Repentance

You must deal with the giants in your life, otherwise they have children. Phil Pringle

A little girl got saved and applied for membership to a church. "Were you a sinner?" she was asked. "Yes," she replied. "Are you still a sinner?" "Yes." "Then what real changes have taken place in your life?" "The best way I can explain," said the little girl, "is that I used to be a sinner running after sin, but now I'm a sinner running away from sin."

Repentance means to stop and turn away from sinning – not just to cut down. The difference is illustrated by the story of the cop who pulled over someone for failing to stop at a stop sign. The man objected that he had slowed right down even if he hadn't come to a complete stop. The cop explained that that wasn't good enough. You had to come to a complete stop. The motorist replied, "Aw, come on officer. There's no difference. Haven't you got anything better to do than pick on innocent people." The cop yanked him out of his car, cuffed his hands behind his back, and started laying into him. "Stop!" the man yelled. The cop grabbed him by the throat and said, "Now, sir, do you want me to stop or just slow down?"

A little girl said: "That horse must be a Christian; it has such a long face."

King Frederick the Great of Prussia was once inspecting a prison in Berlin. One by one, each of the prisoners kneeled before him, claiming that they were innocent. Only one man remained silent. Frederick asked him, "Why are you in this prison?" "Armed robbery, Your Majesty," he replied. "And are you guilty?" asked the king. "Yes, Your Majesty, I am being justly punished." Frederick summoned the jailer, ordered him to release the man immediately, and said, "I do not want him kept in this gaol where he will corrupt all the fine innocent people who occupy it."

Reputation

72-year-old Warren Buffett has a personal fortune estimated to be $30.5 billion (U.S.) – "second only to Bill Gates." He "once raised $210,000 at a charity auction for his 20-year-old wallet, with a stock tip inside." This was because of his reputation.[94]

It takes twenty years to build a reputation and five minutes to ruin it. Warren Buffet

Responsibility

A Christian was talking to a soap manufacturer about his faith. "Don't think much of your Christianity," said the soap man. "It's been around all these years and look at the mess the human race is in." At this point, they passed two or three children playing in the mud at the side of the road. "What about your soap?" replied the Christian. "It's been around longer than

---

[94] *Time Magazine* 10-3-03 p45

Christianity and look at the mess those kids are in."
"Ah," said the soap manufacturer, "my soap is only effective as and when applied." "That's exactly how it is with Christianity," said the Christian.

"I believe that the reason I smoke and drink and my wife is overweight is because we watched TV every day for the last four years." Timothy Dumouchel, who threatened to sue a cable company for providing free cable for four years after he asked that it be cancelled.[95]

He wrecked his car, he lost his job,
And yet throughout his life,
He took his troubles like a man;
He blamed them on his wife.

Revenge

A very big thumbs down to the person or persons who invaded our privacy on September 18, in the early hours of the morning. Thieves are not welcome in our house. Not only did they invade our privacy but they stole a cream nightie from the washing line. I wish only bad karma to you and hope that the bear which is on the front of my nightie, urinates all over you in your sleep. One day someone will steal from you and then you will know just how it feels.[96]

A woman walked into a pharmacy and asked for some arsenic. "Arsenic is a poison. What do want it for?" the pharmacist asked. "To kill my husband because he's having an affair," replied the woman. "But I can't sell you arsenic to kill your husband!" the horrified pharmacist said. The woman opened her

[95] *Time Magazine* 19th January, 2004, p7
[96] Letter from reader to "*Thumbs Up, Thumbs Down*", *The Reporter* 3-10-01, p 10.

handbag taking out a highly compromising photo of her husband with the pharmacist's wife. The pharmacist took one look at the photo and said, "Why didn't you say you had a prescription in the first place?"

Warring factions in Kenya: "One tribal warrior, a bus conductor, declared: 'We have vowed that for every Kikuyu killed, we shall kill two Kalenjins.'"[97] This is why God instituted the law of talion. See Exodus 21:23-25.

Revival

In the mid-1800s in the town of Kells in Northern Ireland, four men met each Saturday night for intense prayer. The whole night was devoted to prayer. Shortly afterwards, there was a powerful revival. Courts adjourned for lack of cases. Gaols were closed for lack of criminals. Policemen formed quartets to sing in churches because they had nothing else to do.

Reward

Two missionaries were returning home after many years of service. As the boat pulled in, there was a brass band. Their first thought was that it was for them, but they quickly realised there was a visiting dignitary. They collected their baggage and booked into a cheap motel. After a while, the man started to cry. "We've served God for many years. We've got no money, no house, and when we return home there's not even anyone to meet us." His wife smiled at him gently and said, "Darling, we're not home yet."

---

[97] *Sunday Mail* 27th January, 2008, p48.

Righteousness

Righteousness is not a long face and a big Bible.

Risk Taking

Isabel and Valerie von Jordan [her sister] escaped the tragedy in Bali and went to Kakadu National Park. Five days later, they were swimming in the moonlight in crocodile infested waters, when Isabel was attacked and killed by a 5m croc. Signs were clearly posted warning about saltwater crocodiles.[98]

A professor faced his class of molecular biology students who were waiting nervously to take their final exam. He said, "I know how hard you have all worked this semester in preparation for this test, and that you all have great plans for the future. You have studied well, and I am certain that you will all pass this exam. Therefore, I am willing to give an automatic B to anyone who decides not to sit for this test." Immediately, a bunch of students jumped to their feet, thanked the professor, and left. "Anyone else want to leave?" asked the lecturer. "I won't offer again." Another student packed up and left the room. The professor then handed out the test. The few remaining students stared at the page before them. It said, "Well done. You have been awarded an A for this subject. Always believe in yourself."

Two caterpillars were perched on a leaf when they saw a butterfly overhead. The first caterpillar said to the second, "It might look like fun, but you'll never get me up in one of those things."

---

[98] *Sunday Mail*, 27-10-02 p3

Sacrifice

A large congregation was surprised one Sunday morning when two men entered their service. Covered in black from head to toe and toting sub-machine guns, one of them declared, "If anyone here is willing to die for Jesus, stay where you are." There was a mass exodus. The deacons, the choir, and most of the congregation, ran for their lives. Only twenty people remained. Smiling up at the preacher, the man who had spoken said, "Well pastor, looks like all the hypocrites have gone. Now it's over to you. Have a nice day!" And the two men turned and left.

You have to leave the first step before you can get to the second step.

As we shook hands and bade each other farewell at the end of the seminar, he looked me straight in the eyes, gripped my hand firmly, and said, "Andrew, when they kill me, it will be for speaking, not for being silent." When, not if.[99]

Jesus is our supreme example of sacrifice. It's clear from Mark 14:32-36 that it was a difficult decision for Jesus to allow Himself to be crucified. He didn't wake up that day excited about His death. It was a tough call; it was a sacrifice.

It had started just like any Sunday. Pastor Cecep Sanabuki led the service at his church, and then travelled with his friend Berty to the airport. Cecep was on his way to attend Bible College classes. Upon arrival at the airport, however, they discovered that all flights had been cancelled due to a security alert. The two men headed for home on their motorbike. Not long into their journey, they came across a roadblock.

---

[99] Brother Andrew in *The Muslim Challenge* p10

Berty tried to reason with the gang of extremists, but to no avail. The mob began to beat him, pulled out his teeth, and eventually cut his throat. Pastor Cecep was also tortured. His charred body was found on a beach two days later, with many deep stab wounds.[100]

A family was in a serious traffic accident. The youngest son, Mike, was seriously injured and needed blood. His big brother, Danny, was only eight years old, but had the same blood type. Danny's Dad explained carefully how important it was for Mike to have blood, and how great it would be if Danny could help out. There was silence for a while, then Danny said, "Yes, Daddy, I'll give my blood so Mike can get better." They put the needle in his vein and drew the blood they needed. Once the needle was back out, Danny looked up at his Dad, and with tears running down his cheeks said, "Daddy, when do I die?" It was only then that his Dad realised that Danny didn't know he was just giving some blood. He thought he was giving his life.

Matthew, a tax collector, is making money hand over fist. Despised by all the people for collaborating with the Romans, he absorbs himself in his world of money. Then one day, Jesus passes by, looks at Matthew, and simply says, "Follow Me." And for one brief moment, Matthew has a dilemma. A split-second image of all his gold and his silver and his house and his possessions. Then he looks at Jesus and realises he's got to make a choice; he can't have both. But there was no comparison. He recognised instantly that he was looking at the True Treasure, the

---

[100] Open Doors letter March 2005 – article on Indonesia.

true riches. And he left everything: He made a sacrifice that turned out to be no sacrifice at all.

Najee just couldn't keep his conversion a secret any longer. With his decision to turn from Islam to follow Jesus, he had found what he had been looking for all his life. And his heart was full beyond anything he had ever felt. His life had been so dramatically transformed he had to tell someone! So one night, Najee told his wife he had become a follower of Jesus. Little did he know it would cost him his life. Najee's wife was a devout Muslim. And she felt a duty to tell her father about Najee's conversion … who in turn shared the news with the local imam. A few days later, Najee's body was found in a sleeping bag … a Bible taped to his body with a single gunshot through the Bible.[101]

Salvation

A Christian was talking to a soap manufacturer about his faith. "Don't think much of your Christianity," said the soap man. "It's been around all these years and look at the mess the human race is in." At this point, they passed two or three children playing in the mud at the side of the road. "What about your soap?" replied the Christian. "It's been around longer than Christianity and look at the mess those kids are in." "Ah," said the soap manufacturer, "my soap is only effective as and when applied." "That's exactly how it is with Christianity," said the Christian.

Here's what happens when people spot a prairie fire coming. They can't escape on the fastest horse. They take a match, light the grass around them. Then they stand in the burned area and are completely

---

[101] Open Doors newsletter 2-2-2009

safe. They can hear the flames roar around them, but they are unafraid. Why? Because the fire has already passed where they stand and they are in no danger. When the fire of God's judgment comes, you can stand where the fire has already been – in Christ. God's judgment was already passed on Him when He was crucified. (See Isaiah 53:5-6)

How can one person die for all? Compare a stainless steel ring with a 24-carat gold ring. They may be exactly the same shape and size, but the gold ring is worth far more. Why? The value lies in the quality of the metal. Since Jesus was God in the flesh, His life was worth far more than that of every human who ever lived. That's why He could pay the price for all.

Satan

If he [Satan] can knock out the head, he can take down the whole body. G. F. Watkins

Did you hear about the dyslexic devil worshipper? He sold his soul to Santa.

I don't play in his [Satan's] playground. If I played in his playground, he'd eat my lunch. Paul Ruzinsky

The devil had a closing down sale and was selling all his tools and devices of destruction. Someone asked him how much he wanted for the wedge of doubt. He said, "It's not for sale; I can get back into business with that anytime."

Satan is known as the accuser of the brethren. But it's a little like being on a small island in the middle of the ocean, with Satan on another island. When he throws mud at you, his island gets smaller, and yours gets bigger. He loses ground, and you gain ground.

In one documentary, a couple were walking through lion country with a native guide. They were totally unarmed, but the guide had instructed them that if charged by a lion, they must not move. They must stand their ground and just look at the big cat. As they were walking along, a lion noticed them and charged with a roar. They stood their ground and it halted a few metres away, backed up and charged again. This process was repeated a number of times, but the trio continued to stand their ground. Eventually the lion gave up and rejoined the pride. Ephesians 6:13 1 Peter 5:8 James 4:7

Two boys face each other. They call each other lots of names, but neither of them actually wants to fight. So one of them draws a line in the dirt and says, "I dare you to cross that line." Now the second boy has a problem. He can't back off, but he can't step over the line. So he draws another line in the dirt and says, "Well, I dare you to cross *that* line." But if one of them calls the other's bluff and crosses the line, the other one has a major problem. He really won't know what to do next. The devil bluffs too, and he knows that if you call his bluff, he'll lose the fight.

Scripture

Reading the Word of God is like eating fish. When you come across some bones just put them aside. Put difficulties aside and read on. Don't throw out the fish with the bones.

Randall Peterson, a retired autoworker, thinks there could be an interest for a new kind of Bible. He sarcastically says that a publisher ought to create an electronic Bible that would allow for editing from the pew. That way individuals and churches could make the Bible say what they want it to say. He says it could be called the "LAME" Bible: "Locally Adaptive

Multifaith Edition" and "could be sold to any church regardless of what it believes."[102]

Do we Christians have time to eat daily, but no time to get into the Word? Do we have time to read the newspaper every day, but not the Bible? Time enough to glue ourselves to the TV set, but no time for the Scriptures? What does all of this say about our values?[103]

Lift your Bible up. It makes the devil nervous. If you really want to make him nervous, open it up. James deMelo

Converted Indian: "I have two dogs living in me – a mean dog and a good dog. They are always fighting. The mean dog wants me to do bad things, and the good dog wants me to do good things. Do you want to know which dog wins? *The one I feed the most!*"

Abraham didn't have a Bible, but he knew God.

An English teacher wrote on the blackboard: "Woman without her man is nothing." Then she asked her Year Ten class to punctuate the sentence correctly. The boys wrote: "Woman, without her man, is nothing." The girls wrote: "Woman: without her, man is nothing." Since the original New Testament was written without punctuation, this highlights the occasional problems in interpreting Scripture.

Vincent Quiroga in Chile found a few pages washed up on the shore after a tidal wave. He read them and wouldn't rest till he got a complete Bible. He became

---

[102] *Our Daily Bread* 27th July, 2008
[103] Earl D. Radmacher – *You And Your Thoughts*

a Christian and devoted his life to distributing the Scriptures in northern Chile.[104]

Seeking God

I was looking for a glass-fronted bookshelf, and decided I might save myself some time and petrol if I used the internet to track one down instead of my car. But results, I discovered, are often more than a little perplexing. On one website, the page was headed: "Products Matching 'Glass Front Bookshelf.'" Naturally, I was hoping to find glass-fronted bookshelves. Instead, out of the twelve possible items for me to select from, there was a vacuum cleaner, an outdoor gazebo, a cello, retractable crowd control barriers, sports bags, a multi-purpose ladder, a baby carriage, and a motorised folding arm awning. God is much more reliable. His promise is that if we search for Him with all our hearts, that's what we'll find. (Jeremiah 29:13)

Self

He is no fool who gives up that which he cannot keep to gain that which he cannot lose. Jim Elliot, martyred by Auca Indians

In a group photo, whose picture do you look for first?

Self-Control

Promises can be hard to keep, especially when it comes to sex. U.S. teens who pledged to remain virgins until marriage had a bit of trouble keeping their word, according to a study of 12,000 adolescents by researchers at Columbia and Yale. In fact, 88% of them went ahead and had premarital sex anyway.

---

[104] Barclay, William *The Daily Study Bible: Timothy, Titus & Philemon* p 201

What's more, those who made a vow of chastity were less likely to use condoms than other teens, contracted sexually transmitted diseases just as often and were less likely to know they were infected. It's difficult for teens to learn safe sex while saying they're not going to have sex, says study co-author Peter Bearman.[105]

Self-Image

If your dog thinks you're the greatest person in the world, don't ask for a second opinion.

[At a college campfire at the end of a beautiful day a blind girl gave thanks.] "I haven't been able to see the beautiful things you have been giving thanks for, but on the other hand, I haven't had to look at the ugly things you have had to look at... More seriously, I thank God for my blindness. You see, I have been blind from birth. I have never seen anything. My eyes are virgin eyes. And do you know what their first sight will be? Jesus Christ! I will see Him when He gives me my new body eternal in the heavens, fashioned like His glorious body."[106]

I am odd-looking. Sometimes I think I look like a Muppet. Angelina Jolie

Selfishness

Egotist: Someone who is usually me-deep in conversation.

Selflessness

Francesco de Pietro Bernadone was the fun-loving son of a wealthy merchant in Assisi. One day, as he was riding his horse, he encountered a dying leper.

---

[105] *Time Magazine* 11th March, 2004, p67
[106] Earl D. Radmacker *You and Your Thoughts*

He was repulsed by the leper's open sores, but suddenly he saw a picture of himself as Jesus saw him. He jumped off his horse, put all his money into the leper's hand, and gently kissed the leper's hand. It was a profound spiritual experience as he died to self and set a foundation in his life to become Francis of Assisi.

After all Paul had been through, his overriding concern was for the churches. See 2 Corinthians 11:22-28.

Self-Scrutiny

Examine your heart. One man didn't know that his heart was in the wrong place till he had an X-Ray.

Self-Will

The spirit of Cain: I'm going to serve God the way I want to and He's going to have to be happy with that, because that's all He's getting. Mark T. Barclay

Selling

A man wanted to be a salesman, but he stuttered very badly. Then he saw an ad for a job as a Bible salesman for the Bible Society, and he decided to apply for it because he believed God would help him to do it. At the interview, they heard him stutter and said, "We're sorry, but there's no way you could do this job with that kind of stutter." "Please," he said. "Just give me a chance." They asked him to leave the room so they could discuss it. When he had gone, one of them said, "I have an idea. Let's just give him fifty Bibles and leave him to it. It'll take him years to sell them." So that's what they did. A week later, the man returned. "I've sold them. Can I have some more." Just at that moment the Executive was in session, so they asked him to come in and explain how he'd done it. "Easy," he said. "I just ask them, 'Would you like to buy a Bible, or would you like me to read it to you?'"

Servanthood

In Japan, if someone is to run the company, they first work on the factory floor for a year or two, even if they're the boss's son.

In ancient times the slave was seen as a tool much like a hammer or shovel, and there were three kinds of tools. Mute, like a shovel; it can't talk or communicate in any way. Inarticulate, like a donkey; it can make a noise but has limited communicative ability. And articulate, like a human being; it can talk. So if you hit your finger with a hammer and got angry you had a perfect right to smash that hammer to pieces. If your donkey didn't move when you wanted it to, you had every right to whip it. And if you didn't like the way your slave looked at you, you had every right to beat him or do whatever you liked to him.

Remember, the ark was built by amateurs; the Titanic was built by professionals.

A healthy body cleans itself, scratches itself, exercises itself, shaves itself, brushes its hair and teeth, feeds itself, waters itself – as well as all the things that go on inside the body to keep it running. The body takes care of itself. More specifically, the members of the body serve other members of the body. And every member of the body is involved in some capacity. No member of the body is superfluous; each one has a purpose. With this in mind, God has designed each member of the body for its unique function.

Sex

Newspaper ad: SEX It's better than mowing your lawn. Let Eddie and David do the mowing, remove rubbish …

The act of intercourse burns about 200 calories, the equivalent of running vigorously for 30 minutes.[107]

A young girl asked her mother, "Mum, how old are you?" "It's rude to ask a woman her age," her mother said. Sometime later, the girl told her friend what her mother had said. "It's easy to find out her age," her friend said. "Just take a look at her driver's licence." The girl did and said to her mother, "Mum, you're 37 years old." "And how did you find that out?" asked her mother. Ignoring the question, the girl added, "And I know why you and Daddy got a divorce." "Is that right?" said her mother. "Why?" "Because," said the girl, "you only got an F in Sex."

The Holy Spirit leaves the room when a married couple has sex, even if they do it without passion to make new virgins for the Kingdom of God. Peter Lombard, theologian (circa 1100-1164)

A man was a keen golfer and left home early to play every Saturday. One weekend, there was a massive downpour so he returned home, undressed and jumped into bed next to his wife. "That's an unbelievable storm," he said. "Yes, I noticed," his wife replied. "Can you believe that my dim-witted husband is actually out there playing golf?"

At this point, dear reader, let me concede one shocking truth. Some young women actually anticipate the wedding night ordeal with curiosity and pleasure! Beware such an attitude! One cardinal rule

---

[107] *Time Magazine* 19th January, 2004, p56

of marriage should never be forgotten: give little, give seldom, and above all give grudgingly.[108]

The definition of dumb: You're on your honeymoon, a beautiful paradise setting, a stunningly beautiful naked wife, and you're tempted by an apple.

I met him, I liked him. I liked him, I loved him. I loved him, I let him. I let him, I lost him. I met her, I wanted her. I wanted her, I asked her. I asked her, she said no. She said no, and I married her, and sixty years later we're still married.

Mother Superior called all the nuns together and said to them, "I must tell you all something. We have a case of gonorrhoea in the convent." "Thank goodness," said an elderly nun at the back. "I'm so tired of chardonnay."

Signs and Wonders

The Pope, commenting on the wealth pouring into the Vatican's coffers said, "The church can no longer say, 'Silver and gold have I none.'" Thomas Aquinas said in response, "Neither can she say, 'In the name of Jesus Christ of Nazareth rise up and walk.'"

One Sunday morning, a cop in a small town was parked at the kerb when he saw a car swerving all over the road. Taking off in hot pursuit, he pulled the driver over, and recognised him as an alcoholic named Frank. The policeman said, "Frank, you're driving all over the place." Frank said, "I'm just trying to get to church, man." Noticing a bottle on the seat next to Frank, the cop asked, "What's that on your seat, Frank?" "It's just water," said Frank. "Give it to me," the cop demanded. He took a whiff. "That's not

---

[108] Ruth Smythers, *Instruction and Advice for the Young Bride* (1894). *Time* 19th January, 2004, p76

water," he said. "That's wine." Frank just looked up to heaven and said, "Wow, He did it again."

Sin

Take a peach out of the refrigerator for a few days and it begins to spoil. Put it back in the fridge, and it doesn't stop decaying, it just slows down the process. "Religion is a refrigerator; it slows up corruption, but it doesn't stop it." Derek Prince

Most of us think that we're fairly good. But it's a bit like a bunch of wart hogs standing around talking about who's the best looking. You'd say, "Hang on guys, it doesn't matter who you think is the best looking. You're all ugly." It doesn't matter how good we think we are compared with someone else. In God's sight we're all sinners.

A little girl got saved and applied for membership to a church. "Were you a sinner?" she was asked. "Yes," she replied. "Are you still a sinner?" "Yes." "Then what real changes have taken place in your life?" "The best way I can explain," said the little girl, "is that I used to be a sinner running after sin, but now I'm a sinner running away from sin."

"Change your course five degrees south to avoid collision," said the Captain. "Change your course five degrees north to avoid collision," came the reply. "This is the Captain speaking. I said to change your course five degrees south." "This is the First Seaman speaking. Change your course five degrees north." "Change your course five degrees south. This is the Captain of a destroyer." "Change your course five degrees north. This is a lighthouse." We can argue with God if we want to, but that doesn't change the fact that each one of us is a sinner.

If you've got an apple tree, nothing you do is going to make it produce avocados; you can't discipline it, reform it, pray for it. None of this works. In the same way, trying out these techniques on the flesh will not produce the fruit of the Spirit.

"Pastor, I want you to hold me accountable. I really need your help." Matt was the youth pastor. A part-timer, he was not in the building much on weekdays. He had made a point to come to the pastor's office that day. Russ at the big desk, looked at Matt sitting across from him. "I found the first pornographic site accidentally," Matt said. He hesitated. "I was looking for something else, and it was just – there. I was stunned by it and I turned the computer off right away, but – later," he confessed, "I went back." "More than once?" "Yes. Several times. But I felt really guilty about it. I've prayed about it. I told my wife. I asked her forgiveness. But I need someone who will help me control this urge to – to look." Russ fidgeted with the keyboard. "What do you want me to do?" "I need someone who'll look me in the eye sometimes and ask if I've kept myself pure." The two men prayed and Matt left. Russ knew he would never initiate the subject with Matt again. How could he? Like Matt's experience, his had started innocently...[109]

Sin is not the expected norm for a Christian. The captain of a ship does not say, "When this ship sinks, this is what you do." He says, "In the event of an emergency..."

Far more people die of mosquito bites than from mad dogs. Yet we guard against mad dogs, but not mosquitoes. Little sins count.

---

[109] Reed, Eric *Leadership – Winter 2001,* p88

Sincerity

A person may sincerely believe their plane won't crash, but their sincerity won't save them if it does. It won't change what actually happens. "Our beliefs – no matter how deeply held – have no effect on reality."[110]

Sincerity is no substitute for the truth.

Small Groups

David used to have a small group. They were called "David's mighty men." They used to invite people around and kill them.

Jethro's advice to Moses: He saw him looking after the people from morning till evening. "Are you nuts? Why are you doing this?" he asked. "The people come to me to hear from God," replied Moses. "You're crazy. You'll wear yourself out, and them." This was because Moses had a big church. So Jethro advised Moses to appoint leaders of tens, fifties, hundreds and thousands. That spread the burden. And that's how Moses started the first small groups. Exodus 18:13-26

Small Things

Every door turns on a small hinge.

Smoking

Stop Smoking Start Repairing ad (Australian Government): In 8 hours excess carbon monoxide is out of your blood; in 5 days most nicotine is out of your body; in 1 week your sense of taste and smell improves; in 12 weeks your lungs regain the ability to

---

[110] Mittelberg, Mark , Lee Strobel, and Bill Hybels *Becoming A Contagious Christian* p.91

clean themselves; in 3 months your lung function has increased by 30%; in 12 months your risk of heart disease has halved; in 1 year a pack-a-day smoker will save over $4,000; in 5 years your risk of a stroke has dramatically decreased.[111]

When comedian George Burns was asked, "What does your doctor think of your smoking at 100?", he said, "My doctor's dead."

Smoking accelerates the ageing of key pieces of a person's chromosomes by about 4.6 years. The effect of obesity is twice as bad, at nine years.[112]

Percentages of cancers caused by smoking: Lung – 84% (men), 77% (women), Mouth and pharynx – 57% (men), 51% (women), Oesophagus – 54% (men), 46% (women), Larynx – 73% (men), 66% (women), Bladder – 43% (men), 36% (women), Kidney – parenchyma – 28% (men), 21% (women), Kidney – pelvis – 55% (men), 48% (women), Pancreas – 24% (men), 19% (women), Stomach – 14% (men), 11% (women), Cervix – 19% (women), Vulva – 40% (women), Penis – 30% (men), Anus – 48% (men), 41% (women).[113]

Sonship

How do you know when someone is part of a person's family? There's a family likeness. That's how you can tell that my children are my children; they look like me. It's the same in God's family. When a person is born again into God's family, God becomes their Father, and they begin to take on His characteristics.

---

[111] *North-West News* 2-3-11 p18

[112] *The Lancet* cited in *Reader's Digest* October 2005 p 27

[113] NSW Cancer Council as tabled in *The Bulletin* 1-8-06 p 18

Angels were created, not generated. I can take some clay and create a piece of pottery, but I can't create a son. My son is generated. He has my genetic stamp on him. When we were born again, we took on the genetic stamp of Almighty God as His children. No longer just as created beings like the angels.

Sowing & Reaping

The following story appears on the internet on a site intended for lawyers: A Charlotte, North Carolina, man bought a case of rare, very expensive cigars and then insured them against … fire. Within a month, having smoked his entire stockpile and having yet to make a single premium payment on the policy, he filed a claim against the insurance company, stating he had lost the cigars in "a series of small fires." The insurance company refused to pay but the man sued – and won. The judge stated that since the man held a policy from the company in which it had warranted that the cigars were insurable, without defining what it considered to be "unacceptable fire" it was obligated to compensate the insured for his loss. Rather than undergo a long and costly appeal, the insurance company accepted the judge's ruling and paid the man $15,000 for the rare cigars he lost in "the fires." When the smoker cashed his cheque, the insurance company had him arrested on 24 counts of arson. With his own insurance claim and testimony from the previous case being used against him, the man was convicted of intentionally burning the rare cigars and sentenced to 24 consecutive one-year terms.[114]

On 3rd February, 1990, in the US, a man apparently attempted to commit armed robbery. Unfortunately, he made five foolish mistakes. 1. His target was a

---

[114] *Sunday Mail* 9-11-97 p58

gun shop. 2. The shop contained a number of firearms customers in a state where a large percentage of the adult population are permitted to carry concealed handguns. 3. He had to walk around a marked police car to get into the shop. 4. A uniformed officer was standing at the counter. 5. The man announced a holdup and began firing his gun, at which point the policeman and the attendant shot him, covered by several customers who had also drawn their guns.

Spiritual Growth

Billy Graham's wife, Ruth Bell Graham, once saw a sign next to the road saying, "End of Construction. Thank you for your patience." Thinking of the significance of those words, she commented that she'd like to have them on her gravestone.

A baby doesn't think when it's hungry, "I'll wait till later till I cry for food. They've got visitors."

Inaction: A brand-new Plymouth Belvedere was buried in a concrete vault under the courthouse lawn in Tulsa, Oklahoma, 15th June, 1957. Fifty years later, as the city celebrated Oklahoma's 100th year as a state, they opened the vault. Unfortunately, water had seeped into the vault and the Belvedere was nothing but a pile of rust.

Spiritual Warfare (Also See Warfare)

If you're going to go to war, you're going to have to have a hatred for your enemy. Stuart Gramenz

It was 1944, World War 2. Sub-Lieutenant Hiroo Onoda of the Imperial Japanese army was ordered to stay on Lubang Island in the Philippines and hold it for the glory of the Emperor. So he did. The following year, the Allies bombed Hiroshima and Nagasaki and the Japanese surrendered. Shortly after, the war ended, but unfortunately he didn't know. He kept on fighting the next year, and the next year, and was still fighting 29 years after the end of World War 2. He was totally unaware that the war had finished long ago. Even when the police searched through the jungle using megaphones to ask him to surrender and stop shooting the locals, he refused to give up. It wasn't until 1974 when they brought in his wartime commanding officer, to order him to surrender, that he finally stopped fighting. Do you know that it's over for Satan? That he's been defeated? Do you apply the victory of the Cross in your daily life?

If you put soldiers in a barracks and leave them there for long enough, they'll eventually start fighting among themselves.

Back in the American Civil War, a soldier was wounded in the arm. Seeing that he was hurt, his commanding officer yelled, "Gimme your rifle, private, and run to the rear!" The private did as he was told, relieved to be headed for safety. But after heading south for only a small distance, he found himself in the middle of another fight. He then ran west and stumbled into another scuffle. So he ran east but found fighting there too. Finally, he retraced his steps to the front lines shouting, "Captain, I need my rifle back. There ain't no rear to this battle!"

Jesus' purpose was to destroy the works of the devil. Jesus is gone but we still have the works of the devil. Whose job is it now? G.F. Watkins

It's been estimated that between 1945 and 1989, around 20 million people were killed in 91 wars. During the same period, there were 208 coups and revolutions. One country (Bolivia) had 192 coups between 1825 and 1981. Ever since God created this planet, it's been a war zone – and right now we're in the middle of a battle.

In December 1940, Major General Richard O'Connor attacked the Italian army stationed in Egypt. What made this so extraordinary was that the British had comparatively few troops whereas the Italians had 250,000 men there. O'Connor attacked anyway and had fewer than 2,000 casualties. In the process they destroyed 10 Italian divisions, took 170,000 prisoners and captured 400 tanks and 850 guns – one of the most remarkable feats of arms in history. The decisive factor in the Italian loss was their low morale – because they weren't happy with the alliance with Germany, and they certainly weren't prepared to die for Mussolini. So they broke and retreated at a crucial moment. Discouragement was the key.

Interestingly enough, the Roman armour was designed to protect the front of the warrior, not the back. Apparently the assumption was that when the enemies were near, the soldiers were moving towards them, not running away.[115]

How do you eat a banana? First, you separate it from the rest of the bunch.

A number of years ago, a movie came out called *The Bear*, and it went something like this: Once upon a time, there was a mummy bear and a baby bear, and they were so happy together. Then one day an accident happened and the mummy bear died, leaving the little baby bear all alone in the world. One day, the poor defenceless baby bear was out minding his own business, when he was spotted by a big,

---

[115] Wagner, C. Peter *Territorial Spirits* p 20-21

mean, hungry mountain lion. The baby bear started to run; he was trapped next to the river, and jumped in. The mean and nasty mountain lion followed him downstream to where the baby bear came ashore at a crossing. The baby bear was trapped again and made a puny, squeaky sound as the mountain lion closed in for the kill. Then suddenly, the baby bear stood to his feet, opened his mouth, and there was a massive great roar. The mountain lion suddenly remembered that he had something else to do, and ran for his life, terrified. How did the little baby bear do that? The cameras panned round, and there standing behind the baby bear was the hugest, most ferocious daddy bear. This is a great picture of allowing the Lord to fight for us. (1 John 4:4)

Standards

Sign in the Red Dog Saloon in Juneau, Alaska: "If our food, drinks and service are not up to your standards, please lower your standards."

Stewardship

Life is like a coin. You can only spend it once, so spend it wisely.

In 1923, seven of the world's most biggest financiers met in Chicago. Between them they controlled more money than the US Treasury. By 1950: New York Stock Exchange president, Richard Whitney, had been released from prison; Charles Schwab had lived on borrowed money for the last five years of his life and died penniless; Jesse Livermore, Wall Street tycoon, committed suicide; wheat speculator Arthur Cutten died bankrupt; president of the Bank of International Settlement, Leon Fraser, committed suicide; presidential cabinet member, Albert Fall, was pardoned and released from prison to die at home;

Ivar Krueger, at the helm of the world's biggest monopoly, committed suicide.

Strategy

Two men hiking in Canada spotted a bear nearby. One took off his boots and put on his running shoes. "You don't really think they will help you to outrun a bear, do you?" sneered his friend. "No, but I only have to outrun you."

Satan: If he can knock out the head, he can take down the whole body. G. F. Watkins

Strength

There are five levels of strength: (a) our spiritual ceiling; (b) our emotional ceiling; (c) our mental ceiling; (d) our social ceiling; (e) our physical ceiling. You will rise to the level of your lowest ceiling. Kong Hee

The real test of strength is through resistance.

Stress

You know you're in trouble if, while being wheeled into Intensive Care, you try to answer your mobile.

It's this distress that we normally mean when we use the term stress. It's such a common problem that it's estimated that "about one-fifth of all prescriptions given to patients in America, the United Kingdom and most other Western countries are for sleeping pills, tranquillisers or anti-depressants. It seems our greatest international drug addiction problem is not one of teenagers taking marijuana or heroin, but middle-agers taking tranquillisers. The comment has been made ... that if all the people on tranquillisers were banned from driving or operating machinery, the world's economy would collapse overnight."[116]

Driving is one source of stress. Researchers conducted a study in San Francisco a number of years ago. Businessmen were asked to wear a pulse counter on their wrists, and at set times during the day to note down their pulse rate and what they were doing at the time. These men were battling deadlines, involved in important business deals, arguing with competitors and generally living at a frantic pace. Yet, the time when they were most stirred up, as measured by their pulse rates, was when driving to and from work.

Peak-hour travellers face more stress than fighter pilots or riot police. So say UK researchers who found that people experience increase in blood pressure and heart rate, as well as a surge in levels of cortisol, a hormone secreted when the body is under pressure. Psychologist David Lewis explains that travellers' brains briefly shut out the outside world – dubbed "commuter amnesia".[117]

It was 28th April, 1988 and flight 243 was en route to Honolulu with 89 passengers. Twenty-three minutes after take-off, a small section of the roof was suddenly torn away. The sudden decompression resulted in the entire top of the aircraft – from behind the cockpit to the forewing – being ripped off. Flight attendant Clarabelle Lansing was sucked right out of the plane to her death. When the captain looked behind him, all he saw was blue sky. Despite everything, an emergency landing was made ten minutes later, with the flight attendant being the only fatality. A full-scale

---

[116] Stanton, Harry *The Stress Factor* p63

[117] *Reader's Digest* March 2005 p 12

investigation was launched. The result? It was determined that the problem was caused by metal fatigue. Metal fatigue is the "progressive, permanent structural damage"[118] that occurs when it is subjected to normal stresses over a prolonged period.

The greatest industrial cost in the USA is executives having heart attacks. Tom Marshall

Submission

Submission can be seen as either a lid or a covering. A lid will hold you down, but a covering will protect you. G. F. Watkins

Surrender should be willing. Just as a wife has to yield herself to her husband on her honeymoon, so also should the church yield to Christ. If Jesus has to come and say, "Give me that!" it's called rape. G.F. Watkins

Success

Einstein was once asked for his formula for success. He replied, "If A is success, I should say the formula is $A = X + Y + Z$, X being work and Y being play." He was asked, "And what is Z?" "Keeping your mouth shut," said Einstein.

If at first you don't succeed, destroy all evidence that you tried.

We must believe in luck. For how else can we explain the success of those we don't like? Jean Costeau

Asked by Spike TV to choose how they measure success, only 3% of men said through their work, while 31% said they did so through their faith in God, 26% through being the best person possible, 22%

---

[118] Wikipedia definition

through their network of family and friends, and 17% through maintaining a balance between home and work.[119]

An enterprising man in Chicago started peddling cheese. His business failed, and he was deep in debt. A Christian friend challenged him by saying, "You don't take God into your business." This altered his whole perspective. He thought if God wants to run the business He can have it. I'll work for Him. He made God his senior partner. It prospered beyond his wildest imagination. He is J.L. Kraft of Kraft Cheeses, the largest cheese company in the world.

Harvard researcher Robert Rosenthal studied how you can make people successful just by labelling them as such. Students were randomly assigned to two groups, "high potentials" and "low potentials". And those singled out as successful … were.[120]

On 10th May, 1996, Jon Krakauer finally reached the summit of Mt Everest. Several of his fellow climbers had died on the way. Later he wrote, "I understood on some dim, detached level that [it] was a spectacular sight. I'd been fantasising about this moment, and the release of emotion that would accompany it, for many months. But now that I was finally here, standing on the summit of Mt Everest, I just couldn't summon the energy to care."

Humorist and television talk-show host Johnny Carson made millions of dollars from his late-night program, "*The Tonight Show*." With all his fortune, his candour and colourful jokes, you might think he would be one of the happiest people around. But in an interview, one of his relatives reported, "Johnny is one

---

[119] *Time Magazine* 23-8-04 p 41
[120] *Reader's Digest* June 2006 p 127

of the saddest people I know. He's someone who's always looking for a good time, but never finding it."[121]

Suicide

34,427 Record number of suicides reported in Japan last year.[122]

From 1982 to 1992, 22,000 Australians suicided – mostly aged between 15 and 24 and mostly young men. More young men are likely to suicide than die of cancer or road accidents.

Superstition

When the phone number 8888-8888, went to auction in China, Sichuan Airlines paid $281,500. In Chinese, eight is a homonym for rich.

In 1647, Christmas festivities were banned by the Puritan leader Oliver Cromwell. He considered feasting and revelry on what was supposed to be a holy day to be immoral.

Have you heard the story that went round in the 70s about how the Russians were conducting scientific experiments in the centre of the earth, and they dropped a microphone down there and heard people screaming and all sorts of foul language? This story spread like wildfire as Christians said excitedly, "Wow, those atheistic Russians have discovered that Hell is *down there*! And they're trying to keep it a secret." Nobody stopped to ask some really obvious questions like: Since the minimum temperature of the earth's core is over 3,500°C, isn't that bad for microphones? AND: Why on earth would they be dropping a microphone down there anyway?

---

[121] Cordeiro, Wayne *Attitudes That Attract Success* p125-126
[122] *Time Magazine* 25-10-04 p 16

Tattoos

By the age of 40, about half of all people with tattoos experience what is termed "tattoo remorse".[123]

Teaching

Learning is the prerogative of the learner. Jennie Bickmore-Brand

Teamwork

I need partners who aren't on the beach drinking lattés while I'm working my tail off trying to catch fish. Shaun Hansen

What two people have in common may bring them together, but what makes them different tells their fortune.[124]

Geese fly in a V-shaped formation when they fly south for the winter. Apparently, the V-shape enables geese to fly at least 71% farther than if they were flying solo. The reason for this is that each bird causes an updraft for the goose behind, which makes flying much easier. Geese that fall out of formation experience wind resistance that slows them down. They need to rejoin the formation as quickly as possible, otherwise they will be unable to keep up with the rest of the flock.

Telephones

Message on an answering machine: "Hi, I'm probably home. I'm just avoiding someone I don't like. Leave a message and if I don't phone back, it's you."

---

[123] *Reader's Digest* November 2006 p 17
[124] *Time Magazine* 30th December, 2002 – 6th January, 2003 p 71

Television

It has been estimated that by the time a person in our society reaches the age of 18 he has watched 25,000 hours of television, including 350,000 commercials. (You know how intellectually stimulating commercials are.)[125] That's more than 21 weeks of solid TV – day and night!

About 20% of children watch more than 4 hours of TV every weekday.[126]

Couples who have a TV in their bedroom make love half as often as those who keep it a TV-free zone.[127]

Temptation

Some Christians ... suppose that God severs fellowship when a believer sins. Actually, a believer sins because he had already broken fellowship with God. He wouldn't have sinned if he had stayed in fellowship with God.[128]

Baboons are inquisitive creatures. In order to catch one in the Kalahari Desert, the bushman digs a hole in solid rock large enough for a baboon's hand to pass through while extended. He does this while making sure the baboon is watching, then drops in some nuts. The baboon is so curious that after the man has gone, he comes down to investigate and puts his hand in the hole to get the nuts. Once his hand is in, the bushman comes running to catch him, because as much as the baboon wants to escape he will not let go of what's in his hand and he cannot get his clenched fist back through the hole.

---

[125] Radmacher, Earl D *You And Your Thoughts*
[126] *Reader's Digest* October, 2006 p 18
[127] *Reader's Digest* January 2007 p 18
[128] Radmacher, Earl D *You And Your Thoughts*

Many Christians have a simplistic concept of temptation that goes something like this: Satan, at a particular moment, flits to our side and whispers "Do it," and we either do or do not, depending upon our spiritual strength at that moment. We might be more consistently victorious in not "doing it" if we realised that there is much more to temptation than the overt, momentary solicitation to evil and that our strength or weakness at that moment is based upon attitudes that have been forming weeks, months, even years prior. We do not fall in a moment; the predisposition to yield to sin has been forming, building, germinating – but not necessarily consciously so. Sin has both a cumulative and a domino effect. Satan plants subtle stimuli, often subliminal ones; he influences an attitude; he wins a "minor" victory – always in preparation for the "big" fall, the iron-bound habit.[129]

Testing, Problems, Difficulties

A young man was studying ornithology [the study of birds] and had a tough professor. When he came for a test, the professor gave him 25 pictures of birds' feet and told him he had to identify which birds they came from. "I'm not going to do this. Nobody could pass this test," exclaimed the exasperated boy. "Then I'll fail you," said the professor. "So fail me," the student replied angrily. "Okay, what's your name?" The student took off his shoes and said, "You tell me."

"I've just left 150,000 people who have no problems at all," said a man. "That's great. Take me to them," replied his friend. "They're in the cemetery."

---

[129] Kohl, D.G. *Sneaky Stimuli and How To Resist Them* (in *Christianity Today*, 31-1-75)

Touch a thistle timidly and it pricks you! Grasp it boldly and its spines crumble.

The Weaver
My life is but a weaving
Between my Lord and me;
I cannot see the colours,
He worketh steadily.
Oft times He weaveth sorrow,
And I in foolish pride
Forget He sees the upper,
And I the underside.
Not till the loom is silent
And the shuttles cease to fly;
Will God unfold the canvass
And explain the reason why
The dark threads were as needful
In the Weaver's skilful hand;
As the threads of gold and silver
In the pattern He has planned.

Your most unhappy customers are your greatest source of learning. Bill Gates

Circumstances don't make a man, they reveal him. Like teabags, our real strength comes out when we get into hot water.[130]

The fruit tree is never so close to the gardener as when he has the knife in his hands.

Thankfulness

Thanking God is the purest expression of faith. Derek Prince

Once upon a time there was a king who went hunting game with his friend. As the king shot the arrow, his

---

[130] Petersen, J. Allan *The Myth Of The Greener Grass*

thumb came off. His friend said, "Praise God because He's in control." The king was furious and threw his friend in gaol. Sometime later, the king was hunting when he ventured into a distant land where he'd never been before. Suddenly he was surrounded by cannibals. They tied him up and were ready to cook him when they saw the hand with no thumb. "No perfect, no cookie," said the chief, and they let him go. He went back to his friend and apologised. "You were right. Not having a thumb saved my life." His friend said, "Praise God that I have been in gaol for so long." "How can you praise God?" the king asked. His friend replied, "If I hadn't been in gaol, I would have been hunting with you. And look: two thumbs."

Thinking / Thoughts

Harvard researcher Robert Rosenthal studied how you can make people successful just by labelling them as such. Students were randomly assigned to two groups, "high potentials" and "low potentials". And those singled out as successful … were.[131]

Three soldiers were captured by the enemy and sentenced to be shot. As the firing squad aimed, one shouted, "Avalanche!" The firing squad looked round and the soldier escaped. As they aimed again, another yelled, "Flood!" They looked round again and the second soldier escaped. As they aimed again, the third soldier shouted, "Fire!"

To steal ideas from one person is plagiarism; to steal from many is research.

A conclusion is the place where you got tired of thinking.

---

[131] *Reader's Digest* June 2006 p 127

Deliberate thinking is for doing better than just coping. Everyone can run, but an athlete runs deliberately and is trained for that purpose.[132]

I can't stop a bird from flying over my head, but I sure can stop him from making a nest in my hair! John Wesley

Time

Great men never complain about lack of time. Alexander the Great and John Wesley accomplished everything they did in 24 hour days.

The sooner you fall behind, the more time you'll have to catch up.

If you want work well done, select a busy man – the other kind has no time. Elbert Hubbard

We should give of our time liberally for Him. If one lives to be 70 years of age and is the average person, he spends 20 years sleeping; 20 years working; 6 years eating; 7 years playing; 5 years dressing; 1 year on the telephone; 2½ years smoking; 2½ years in bed; 3 years waiting for somebody; 5 months tying shoelaces; 2½ years for other things; (incl. 1½ years in church).

Those who make the worst use of time most complain of its shortness. La Bruyère, French novelist.

A Day in the Life of the Human Machine. If you happen to be an adult of about average weight, here's what you do in 24 hours: Your heart beats 103,689 times. Your blood travels 270 million kilometres. You breathe 23,040 times. You inhale 13 cubic metres of air. You eat 1.7 kilos of food. You drink 1.3 kilos of liquids. You lose in weight 3.5 kilos of waste. You

---

[132] De Bono, Edward *Six Thinking Hats* p 11

perspire 1 litre. You give off 30 degrees Celsius. You turn in your sleep 25-30 times. You speak 48,000 words. You move 750 major muscles. Your nails grow .015 mm. Your hair grows .5mm. You exercise 7,000,000 brain cells. (It pays to take care of the machine... There are no replacement parts for sale!)[133]

To realise the value of one year, ask a student who failed a grade. To realise the value of one month, ask a mother who gave birth to a premature baby. To realise the value of one week, ask the editor of a weekly newspaper. To realise the value of one hour, ask the lovers who are waiting to meet. To realise the value of one minute, ask a person who missed the train. To realise the value of one second, ask a person who just avoided an accident. To realise the value of one millisecond, ask the person who won a silver medal in the Olympics.

62%: Percentage of people who say they are sometimes or often too busy to sit down to eat. 35%: Percentage of people who say they eat lunch at their desk.[134]

Over their lifespan, women spend nearly three years getting ready to leave the house. Before a big night out, women typically spend 22 minutes showering, 7 minutes moisturising, 23 minutes doing their hair, 14 minutes on make-up, and 6 minutes dressing.[135]

Charles Schwab, chairman of the Bethlehem Steel Company, asked a management consultant to give him advice on how he could better manage his time. The management consultant, Ivy Lee, told Schwab

[133] *The Scholastic*
[134] *Time* 11-10-04 p 20
[135] *Reader's Digest* February 2008 p 18

that each evening he should write down the six most important things he had to do the next day and list them in the order of importance. When Schwab asked Lee how much he owed him for his advice, Lee told him to use the plan for a few months and send him a check for whatever Schwab felt the advice was worth. Schwab sent Lee a check for $25,000 — a significant amount of money in those days.[136]

Studies have shown that leaders fail because of poor delegation more than from any other cause.[137]

Asked by a woman what he would do with his time if he knew he would die at midnight the next day, John Wesley replied, "Why madam, just as I intend to spend it now. I would preach this evening at Gloucester, and again at five tomorrow morning: after that I would ride to Tewkesbury, preach in the afternoon, and meet the societies in the evening. I would then go to Martin's house, who expects to entertain me, talk and pray with the family as usual, retire to my room at 10 o'clock, commend myself to my heavenly Father, lie down to rest, and wake up in Glory."

We can be proud of our past and we can hope for our future, but we can only live in the present. Richard Koch

Timing

God's will and God's timing: I always like to say that my wife and I have complementary ministries – she likes to cook and I like to eat. One of her portfolios is the Ministry to the Interior. To my mind, she has an extraordinary ability. If the cooking were left up to me,

---

[136] *Ministry Advantage: Organising & Delegating* p 10
[137] Ministry Advantage, *Organising and Delegating* p 45

we would have burnt potatoes, raw meat and cold peas. But she has the ability to cook a baked dinner and time it so that everything hits the table hot and cooked just right. And it's all about timing; and if the timing isn't right, you don't get a meal that's good.

On 3rd February, 1990, in the US, a man apparently attempted to commit armed robbery. Unfortunately, he made five foolish mistakes. 1. His target was a gun shop. 2. The shop contained a number of firearms customers in a state where a large percentage of the adult population are permitted to carry concealed handguns. 3. He had to walk around a marked police car to get into the shop. 4. A uniformed officer was standing at the counter. 5. The man announced a holdup and began firing his gun, at which point the policeman and the attendant shot him, covered by several customers who had also drawn their guns.

A woman rang her husband on his mobile phone. "Where are you?" she asked. "I'm at work in my office, of course. Where do you think I am?" "Well I know you're not at work." "Why would you think that?" "Because you work at the World Trade Centre and I'm watching the footage showing the buildings collapsing." He was in a motel room with another woman.

The most important thing that ever happened to this planet was the coming of Jesus. You'd think that God would be in a real hurry. But Jesus was a full-term baby. Conception, development, birth, growth …

Titles

Research conducted by a leading compensation technology firm found that among employees planning to leave their companies, a majority felt they were underpaid. Fewer than 20 percent of them, however, were receiving less than the industry standard for their duties. Bill Coleman, of Salary.com, believes that many unhappy workers are overtitled rather than underpaid. Some companies give employees lofty titles even though their job responsibilities have not increased. In time, employees feel they deserve more money than their actual duties merit. "When it comes to salary," Coleman says, "it's what you do, not what you're called, that counts."[138]

Tongue

The bone of contention is the jaw bone.

If you never stop talking, you won't learn anything new because you've heard it all before.

The tongue is the ambassador of the heart.

A man walked past a pet shop with a parrot outside. The parrot called him over and said, "Gee, you're ugly!" The next day, the same thing happened, so the man went in and complained to the manager. The manager apologised and promised to talk to the parrot. The next day, the man was walking past and the parrot called him over again. When he got close, the parrot said, "You know."

One good thing about a compliment is that it doesn't cost a cent more than it used to. Al Bernstein

You will never stamp out a church grapevine, so feed it with the right information.

Don't be like New Jersey's former governor, Robert B. Meyner. One restaurant owner put a picture of him in the window. He had his mouth open, and

---

[138] *Our Daily Bread*, September 1, 2008

immediately above was a sign saying, "Open 24 hours a day."

It's pretty difficult to put your foot in your mouth if you keep it shut.

"The boneless tongue, so small and weak
Can crush and kill," declares the Greek.
"The tongue destroys a greater horde,"
The Turk asserts, "than does the sword."
"The tongue can speak a word whose speed,"
Say the Chinese, "outstrips the steed."
While Arab sages this impart:
"The tongue's great storehouse is the heart."
From Hebrew wit the maxim sprung,
"The feet should slip, ne'er let the tongue."
The sacred writer crowns the whole:
"Who keeps his tongue doth keep his soul."

Four pastors went on a fishing trip. After they'd come ashore and were sitting around the camp fire, one of them suggested that they each confess a secret sin. They all agreed, and the first one said, "Well, I sometimes go down to the track and place a bet on the horses. So that's my secret sin." The second one said, "Mine is that I have an uncontrollable temper. I get so mad at my wife that I blow my stack and hit her." The third preacher said, "I've kept this a secret for years, but I can't resist having a few whiskies after a tough meeting with the elders." There was a long silence as the three preachers looked expectantly at the fourth pastor. Finally, he said, "Well, I guess it's my turn. My sin is gossip. And I can't wait to get home to tell everyone what you've said."

If you haven't struck oil in ten minutes stop boring.

Einstein was once asked for his formula for success. He replied, "If A is success, I should say the formula is A = X + Y + Z, X being work and Y being play." He was asked, "And what is Z?" "Keeping your mouth shut," said Einstein.

A married couple, both 60 years old, were celebrating their thirty-fifth wedding anniversary. A fairy appeared to congratulate them and granted them each one wish. The wife wanted to see the world. The fairy waved her wand, and hey presto, the wife had tickets in her hand for a world cruise. Next, the fairy asked the husband what he wanted. He said, "I wish I had a wife thirty years younger than I am." The fairy waved her wand, and hey presto, he was ninety years old.

A gossip is one who talks about you to others; a bore is one who talks to you about himself; a brilliant conversationalist is one who talks to you about yourself. Lisa Kirk

I hate to spread rumours; but what else can you do with them? Amanda Lear

Never tell anyone anything that you're not prepared for everyone to know.

To sit and discuss the issues and the person causing them, is not considered gossip or wrong when it is being dealt with by leadership. Gossip is when people discuss a matter or a person, but they are not part of the solution and do not possess the authority to resolve the issue. Malicious gossip is when people talk about others to purposely do them harm. Mark T. Barclay

A woman was standing in line at the supermarket check-out. In her trolley, she had cleaning supplies as well as a mop and a broom. Sighing and fidgeting, she was clearly in a hurry and frustrated with the length of time the queue was taking. When the clerk called out for a price check she said loudly, "I think we'll all be lucky to get home before Christmas!" "Don't worry, ma'am," the cashier replied. "There's a good wind out there. With that new broom you'll be home quick as a flash."

The nice thing about egotists is that they don't talk about other people. Lucille Harper

"Mum," said the little boy, "if I promise to be good, can I have five dollars?" "Why can't you be good for nothing like your father?" his mother replied.

A policeman asked the driver of a speeding car, "Can you explain why you were doing thirty over the speed limit?" The man replied, "Your radar must be broken. My cruise control was set way below that." "Darling, you know better than that," said the man's wife. "Our cruise control hasn't worked for ages." As the officer wrote out a ticket, the man snarled at his wife, "Don't you ever know when to keep quiet?" His wife smiled and said, "Just be grateful that your radar detector went off when it did." As the officer was writing out another ticket for an illegal detector, the man yelled at his wife, "Please! Be quiet!" The officer frowned and said, "I notice that you're not wearing your seat belt." "I took it off when I pulled over," said the driver. "But dear," said his wife, "You never wear your seat belt." Seeing the officer write out his third ticket, the driver yelled, "Good grief, woman! Please shut up!" The policeman shook his head and asked, "Is that how your husband always talks to you?" "No," said the woman, "Only when he's had a lot to drink."

"What's a monologue, Dad?" asked the boy. "That's a conversation with your mother, son."

Secret: Something you tell to one person at a time.

The best way to save face is to keep the lower part shut.

In 1987, when Pope John Paul II went to Miami, one man thought he'd make some money by selling T-shirts with the phrase "I saw the Pope" in Spanish. But instead of saying *el Papa* (which means the Pope), he said *la Papa* which meant that the T-shirt read, "I saw the Potato."

Apparently, we speak over nine million words a year.

Light travels faster than sound. That's the reason most people appear to be bright till you hear them speak.

Tongues

Jackie Pullinger, author of *Chasing The Dragon*, went to the walled city of Kowloon in Hong Kong to minister to the Triad gang members. Even when she was baptised in the Holy Spirit nothing happened in her ministry till she committed herself to speaking in tongues every day for fifteen minutes – by the clock. After about six weeks of this, she found new power in her evangelism, and people were much more open to receiving Christ.

Touch

A US study of rabbits on high-cholesterol diets were perplexed to find one group lived about 60 per cent longer than the other on the same food. The difference? The longer-living bunnies were fed by an assistant who cuddled and talked to them.[139]

---

[139] *Reader's Digest* June 2005 p 164

Tradition

A New Zealander went into a fish and chip shop and said, "$5 worth of fush and chups please." "You're a Kiwi, mate," said the Australian. "Yeah, how'd you know?" "It's the accent, mate. Gives you away every time." The New Zealander went home and practised saying, "Fish and chips." A month later he went back to the fish and chip shop and said, "$5 worth of fush and chups please." Again, the Australian said, "You're a Kiwi, mate." "Yeah, how'd you know?" "It's the accent, mate. Gives you away every time." The New Zealander went home and practised again; he even got lessons. A month later he went back to the fish and chip shop and said, "$5 worth of fish and chips please." "You're a Kiwi, mate," said the Australian. "Yeah, how'd you know?" "The fish and chip shop closed three weeks ago. This is a stationery store."

A guard faithfully stood each day at his post. One day, a visitor inquired why he was standing in that exact spot. The guard scratched his head and replied, "I don't know. These are my orders." So the visitor asked the captain of the guard. Again, he received the reply, "I don't know. These are my orders." So the captain asked the king why the sentry was posted in that place, but even the king could not answer. So the king asked his advisors. A hundred years earlier, Catherine the Great planted a rosebush there and the sentry was posted to guard it. Although the rosebush had died eighty years earlier and Catherine the Great was long gone, the sentry still stood guard. Isn't it true that the church sometimes sets something in place, which originally serves a good purpose, and a couple of centuries later, we're still doing it, and nobody even knows the reason why? It's past its use-by date.

The seven last words of the church are, "We've never done it that way before." Ralph Neighbour

Transformation

An atheist was taunting a converted alcoholic. "You don't really believe those Bible miracles such as where Jesus changed water into wine, do you?" "Why not?" replied the believer. "Come to my place and I'll show you how Jesus changed beer into chairs, carpets, and a pool table!"

Farmer Brown and his family had lived out west all their lives, but they had to go to the big city to view some documents. So they loaded up the utility truck and headed to the city. They pulled up outside a massive building and the farmer said to his family, "Stay here. I won't be long." Little Johnny said, "Aw, Dad, can't I come too?" "All right," said the farmer. "But the rest of you stay in the ute." Father and son got out of the truck, and up the steps to the front entrance, when the doors suddenly opened. "Wow, did you see that Dad?" asked the little boy. "The doors just opened by themselves." "Yeah, ya never know what they've got in the city, son." So they wandered around, marvelling at all the things in the building. The farmer asked for directions and the clerk pointed at the lift door. They'd never even seen an elevator before, so they went and stood in front of it, not quite knowing what to make of it. Next thing an old woman came along, got in the lift, and the door shut. A couple of minutes later, the door opened again, and out stepped a beautiful young woman. An old woman went in, and a beautiful young woman came out. The farmer turned to his son, "Quick son, go get your mother." There's a theological truth in this: God isn't interested so much in changing us, as He is in exchanging us at the cross.

Treasure

A wealthy man was giving a pastor a guided tour of his property. He pointed north and said, "I own everything for as far as you can see." Then he pointed east, south, and west, each time repeating, "I own everything for as far as you can see there too." The preacher responded, "That's impressive. But," he added, pointing upward, "How much do you own up there?"

In the early gold rush days in Australia in the 1850s, the discovery of gold had a profound effect on the country; it transformed it. People got excited. And in two years the population of Victoria exploded from 77,000 to 540,000. The prospect of finding a treasure in the ground generated enthusiasm and excitement.

Trials

If you want the rainbow, you've got to put up with the rain.

When the world knocks you down to your knees, it's the perfect place to pray. Alan Beardall.

There's no sense in advertising your troubles; there's no market for them.

If you can't handle the heat, you'd better get out of the kitchen. Harry Truman

Problems only exist for solutions. Henry Ford

If a butterfly is assisted in emerging from its chrysalis, then it doesn't develop the strength in its wings to be able to fly.

A woman was dying in a poor-house. When the doctor visited her, he found her very bright and happy. "How can you be so happy?" he asked. "That's easy. I just keep thinking about the move into my heavenly mansion."

What has the potential to destroy you, also has the potential to become the seeds of your greatness. Ivan Herald

Bible College lecturer to his students: "In this Bible College you will learn your lesson and then go out and do it. In God's Bible College, you will go through your experience and then learn your lesson."

You will experience problems if you are a threat to the devil. James deMelo

In January, we joined a gym. Most of the equipment looked like it had been designed by the Marquis de Sade. I started on the leg press machine doing 40kg. I kept working at it till I reached 160kg. I stayed on this weight for about 4-6 weeks then suddenly started to increase again. By the end of May, I was leg pressing 200kg. There can be no increase in strength without resistance and opposition.

If you're in a boat off-shore, coming into the beach, sometimes you'll be on the crest of the wave, and sometimes you'll be in the trough. You can't always be on the crest, but that doesn't mean you're not heading for the shore.

When you're mountain climbing, you can rest on the plateaux. But the real progress is made when you face the mountain, tough it out, and head for the peak. Real growth comes in times of testing.

All sunshine makes a desert. Arab proverb

Super heroes reveal themselves to be super heroes in the midst of super challenging situations where they must draw upon super powers to overcome super problems. Otherwise they look just like ordinary people.

The apostle Paul was one who suffered tremendously for the gospel: shipwrecked three times, stoned, beaten with rods three times, in constant danger, jailed, rejected by his own countrymen, experiencing many times of nakedness, hunger, thirst, fasting, fear, destitution, and sleeplessness. He said, "For I consider that the sufferings of this present time are not worthy to be compared with the glory which shall be revealed in us." (Romans 8:18) Now that's a faith perspective!

Burdens: We need the weight of the atmosphere. It is necessary for our bone density. Astronauts lose bone density, while in space, because of weightlessness.

Trust & Trusting

"Having your faith in somebody voided makes it virtually impossible to recover," says Louise Young, a trust researcher and professor of marketing at the University of Technology Sydney. "People can redeem themselves only to a relatively small degree."[140]

Only one in three couples now have a joint bank account.[141]

Trusting God

Faith looks ahead with courage, while unbelief looks back with complaint. Roy Funu

---

[140] *Reader's Digest* June 2005 p 42
[141] *Reader's Digest* October, 2006 p 18

A man was walking on a pitch black night when he fell over a cliff. On the way down, he managed to grab hold of a small tree sprouting out of the side of the precipice. Desperately he began to call out for help and a voice answered, "What do you want?" "I'm stuck down here holding on to a tree." he replied. "I can't hold on too much longer. Can you help me?" "Yes," came the reply. "Who are you ?" the man asked. "I'm God," replied the voice. "What do you want me to do?" asked the man. "Let go of the tree." For a while there was silence. Then the man called out and said, "Is there anyone else up there?"

Jonah had to trust in God, because there are only two ways out of a fish.

Depend on the rabbit's foot if you will, but remember it didn't work for the rabbit. R. E. Shay.

Truth

A man charged with murder bribed a friend on the jury to hold out for a verdict of manslaughter. The jury was out for a long period of time, but finally brought in a verdict of manslaughter. Upon visiting the prisoner the following week, the friend was thanked. "You must have had a tough time getting them to vote for manslaughter." "Tough is right," replied the friend. "The other eleven wanted to acquit you."

82.7% of all statistics are made up on the spot.

A medical student was asked how much of a certain drug should be administered to a patient. "Five grams," said the young man. A minute later he raised his hand and said, "Professor, I would like to change my answer to that question." The professor looked at his watch and said, "Too late. Your patient has been dead for forty seconds." Sincerity is no substitute for the truth; we need to make sure we have the truth *now*. It will be too late to change our minds in eternity.

God has ways of letting lies catch up on you. A pastor had had a very busy program and so decided to take the Sunday off and go and play golf. So he contacted his elders and told them he had been invited to preach in a neighbouring city and he would be away Sunday, and so he arranged for someone to take his place. The following Sunday came and the Lord looked down as the pastor was about to take his first swing. Speaking to an angel, he said, "Watch this. I'll teach him a lesson." The pastor swung and his first shot was a hole in one. Then he lined up again and again, and each time got a hole in one. After a while the angel could contain himself no longer. "Lord," he said. "I thought you were going to teach him a lesson." The Lord smiled and said, "Think about it. He's never had a hole in one in his life before and now he's got nine in a row. And who can he tell?"

One week, a preacher asked his congregation to read the Gospel of Mark, chapter 17, for the following Sunday. When the day came, he asked, "So, how many of you did your homework and read Mark 17?" A lot of hands shot up. "Sadly," said the minister, "there are only sixteen chapters in Mark. This morning I am preaching on honesty."

A 95-year-old who had married a much younger woman, visited his doctor, and told him that they were expecting a baby. "Here's a story that might interest you," said the doctor. "An absent-minded man went on safari, but he accidentally picked up his golf club instead of his rifle. Suddenly, he was charged by a lion. He aimed his golf club at the lion and fired, killing the animal immediately." "Impossible," cried the old man. "Somebody else must have killed the lion!" "That's exactly right," said the doctor.

On the way to school, three boys decided to go fishing and stayed so long they became very late. When they arrived, the teacher asked them why they were so late. They said that they'd had a flat tyre. But the teacher suspected something was amiss, and handed each of them a blank sheet of paper saying, "You sit over there, you over there, and you over there. Now I want you each to write down which tyre was flat."

If you asked a rocket scientist how a rocket worked, he might describe the need for a certain amount of thrust to break free of gravity, the trajectory, the effect of the gravitational pull of the sun and the moon, and lots more. You would probably end up saying, "I'll just take your word for it." Just because you don't understand something doesn't mean it isn't true.

A grandmother was looking after her two little grandchildren, a 7-year-old girl, and a 5-year-old boy. And boy, were they naughty! When it came time for their mother to pick them up, the little girl said, "Are you going to tell Mummy?" The grandmother replied, "No, I'm not. But if she asks me, I can't tell a lie." The little boy looked up to her and said, "Why not? I'm only five, and I can lie great."

Professor Jeff Hancock asked 30 subjects to keep a communications diary for a week and made them fess up to how often they fibbed during the course of their interactions, be they in person, on the phone, via e-mail or instant message. (Earlier research found that people lie in about a quarter of their daily interactions.) What Hancock discovered was that lies made up a whopping 37 per cent of phone conversations and 27 per cent of face-to-face interactions, whereas the computer-assisted technologies kept people more honest. Lies made up only 21 per cent of instant messaging and just 14 per cent of e-mails. Hancock believes that because e-mails leave a record, many would avoid including lies in them.[142]

A woman rang her husband on his mobile phone. "Where are you?" she asked. "I'm at work in my office, of course. Where do you think I am?" "Well I know you're not at work." "Why would you think that?" "Because you work at the World Trade Centre and I'm watching the footage showing the buildings collapsing." He was in a motel room with another woman.

Unbelief

LONDON: A Baptist minister has told his flock to put aside the Bible ... and concentrate on TV's *Eastenders*. The Rev. Guy Lawrence says the goings on with Dirty Den and Co are a better guide to everyday living than obscure passages from the New Testament. The new approach has proved a hit with the congregation.[143]

A man and his dog were walking the beach when they came upon another visitor to the beach. The owner of the dog was proud of his dog's newly mastered feat, so he said to the visitor, "Watch this!" whereupon he tossed a piece of driftwood far out into the sea and the dog immediately ran on top of the ocean, fetched the wood, and ran back. The visitor just shook his head in disbelief. Whereupon the owner repeated the

---

[142] *Australian Reader's Digest* May 2004 p162
[143] *Sunday Mail* 31-5-87

procedure twice. Finally he asked the visitor, "Did you notice anything unusual?" The visitor responded, "Your dog can't swim, can he?"

November 1837: Distinguished British physicist, Dionysius Lardner, proved mathematically with indisputable equations, that it was impossible for a steamship to get to New York on a non-stop voyage. Proof of his assertion arrived in New York, in printed form, 24th April, 1838, aboard the *Sirius* – the first ship to cross the Atlantic by steam only.

Value

Imagine a bicycle on sale at around $300. Suppose the world's oil reserves were totally exhausted, and the motor car became obsolete overnight. How much is that $300 bicycle going to sell for now? $500? $700? $1000? $1500? Whatever it is, you can rest assured that it won't stay at $300. It will now be valued at much more because, whereas before many people weren't interested in that bike, now everyone needs it because it's the only way they can get around. It's the same bike, but a value has been set on it from outside itself. Whereas previously, you might say, "You're kidding! $300 for a bike?" Now you're bragging: "Hey I got it for only $700!" It's the same with us. We are the same people whatever our works, but God has set a value on us according to His own love, and not according to our works.

When God measures a person, He places the measuring-tape around the heart and not the mind. Augustine

Values

A young man applied for a job as an architect. They called him up and asked him to come in. When he

232

did, they offered him the job at $150,000. He went to sign the agreement and was told, "You are expected to look after your clients, wine them, dine them, and take them to girlie places. I hope your wife will understand." The architect said, "No thanks." "What! This is the opportunity of a lifetime." "No thanks, I'm not willing to sell my values for $150,000." A few days later, he got a promotion from his current boss.

One dark and stormy night, a gang of thieves broke into a jewellery store, but strangely, they didn't steal a thing. They were on a mission with a difference. They carefully went through the whole shop and switched all the price tags. Cheap trinkets had high prices, and valuable jewellery had low prices. Then they left. The next day, the staff came in, and because the thieves had been so careful, nobody noticed they'd even been there. Customers spent huge amounts of money buying cheap junk, while others paid a couple of dollars for jewellery worth thousands of dollars. Unbelievable? Then think about this. Someone has switched the tags on our planet. The things that are really precious are deemed unimportant, whereas insignificant things are considered valuable. In fact, we are continually bombarded with a different set of values from what the Bible teaches.

Victorious Living

Victorious living is a struggle between the old man and the new man. It's like a dog-fight. If you feed one, it becomes strong. Starve the other it becomes weak.

A wealthy man wanted to help someone in need. So one day, he found a homeless man, opened a new bank account in his name, and deposited $1million into the account. When he told the man what he had done, the man said, "I don't believe it. A million dollars? If I draw any of that money out, I could be in serious trouble." Despite having all that wealth at his disposal, he continued to live as a pauper. Isn't that what so many Christians do too? Even with all the provisions made available through the cross, they still live as spiritual paupers.

The enemy is behind us. The enemy is in front of us. The enemy is to the right and the left of us. They can't get away this time. General Douglas MacArthur

Robert Louis Stevenson had not enjoyed a single day of good health in fourteen years. One day, when he had been forced to set aside his writing because of violent coughing and hacking, his wife said to him, "I suppose you're going to tell me it's a glorious day." As he watched the sunlight streaming through the window, he said, "Yes, because I refuse to allow a row of medicine bottles to form the circumference of my world."

The winner is always part of the answer. The loser is always part of the problem. The winner always has a program. The loser always has an excuse. The winner says, "Let me do it for you." The loser says, "That's not my job." The winner sees an answer for every problem. The loser sees a problem in every answer.

Vigilance

The 4,000-mile-long Great Wall of China was built to keep out invaders from the north. The first wall was constructed by Shi Huangdi, the first emperor of China, who lived between 259 and 210 BC. But in AD 1644 the Manchus broke through the Great Wall and overran China. They did this by bribing a general of the Ming dynasty to open the gates.[144]

Vision

Focus always creates blindness. Tom Moffett

An eagle can see a mouse from a mile above the earth.

Don't share your ninety centimetre vision with a one centimetre mind. If you ever share your vision with a one centimetre mind, they will always create it smaller. James deMelo

Double vision will cause headaches. James deMelo

Once upon a time, when Spain controlled the territory both sides of the Straits of Gibraltar, they stamped the two Pillars of Hercules (what they called the two promontories of rock) on their coins, and a scroll bearing the words, "No more beyond." Meaning there ain't nothing else out there. Then came the discovery of the New World, and with it the realisation that there was in fact something else out there. So they changed the coins to read, "More beyond." Mostly our limits don't come from God, but from within us. As you look at your life, has fear or some other negative thing burned into your life, "No more beyond"? Or are you convinced that there is indeed more beyond, and that you're going to reach out for it?

A swimmer asked his coach, "When will I get my Olympic gold medal?" The coach took him to the pool, held his head under water until he began to struggle. Then he said, "This is your answer." He went on to tell him that he'd get his gold medal when

---

[144] *Our Daily Bread* 31st January, 2009

he wanted to be the best in his sport as desperately as he wanted to get his breath of air.

Imagine doing a jigsaw puzzle without the picture on the front. You have to be able to see what you're aiming for.

In one church, the elders spent two board meetings from 7pm to midnight discussing whether to change the bulbs in the sanctuary from 60 watts to 100 watts.

Fulfilling a vision takes concrete planning. A little boy was repeatedly invited and coaxed to take a handful of sweets from a jar. After failing to gain the boy's cooperation, the storekeeper finally reached in and pulled out a handful. Outside, his mother asked, "Why didn't you take the sweets when they were offered?" "I could have," replied the little boy. "But the storekeeper's hand is bigger than mine."

Waiting

God promised Abraham a son; he had to wait twenty-five years. God promised Joseph a position of authority; he had to wait thirteen years before it happened. David had to wait about the same time till he was king.

Warfare

A man was asked this question in training for Vietnam: "Are you prepared to kill?" When he got there he realised the question should have been, "Are you prepared to die?"

A good general will penetrate the brain of his enemy. Victor Hugo

It has been estimated that the world has been at peace for only 8% of the last 3,000 years of recorded history.

Between 1945 and 1988, about 20 million people died in 91 wars.

As one Austrian military expert remarked in his analysis of Helmuth von Moltke's three short and victorious wars, "Prussia has conclusively demonstrated that the strength of an armed force derives from its *readiness* ... A ready army is twice as powerful as a half-ready one.[145]

Napoleon had observed that the most important characteristic of a great commander is calm ... But this tranquillity must be accurately transmitted to his subordinate commanders, so that it is not mistaken for denial, inertia, or incomprehension.[146]

Weakness

Every time Satan knocks at the door, I let Jesus answer. (Derek Prince relating what an old lady replied when asked the secret of her victorious life.)

My call is before any of my faults, and my call is greater than any of my faults. Tom Moffatt

The key to my ministry is my deficiencies. ... Your deficiencies will open the doors to your ministry. Nick Vujicic

Will Of God

There is a prerequisite for knowing the will of God; and it's this – being willing to do it ... God does not say to you, "I'll show you My will and then I'd like you to decide if you'd like to do it." He does not reveal His will so that you can speculate on it, so that you can think about it, or so you can take it to a church board

---

[145] Mosier, John *Grant* p77 citing Field Marshall Heinrich Hess as quoted in *The Franco-Prussian War* by Geoffrey Wawro
[146] Mosier, John *Grant* p95

meeting and vote on it. God reveals His will to people who are committed to do it no matter what it is. Bob Orr

Martin Luther's close friend, Frederick Myconius, became extremely ill in 1540. Since he had lost the ability to speak, it was clear that he would soon die. He informed Luther in a farewell letter, to which Luther replied, "I command you in the name of God to live because I still have need of you in the work of reforming the church... The Lord will never let me hear that you are dead, but will permit you to survive me. For this I am praying, this is my will, and may my will be done, because I seek only to glorify the name of God." Not only did Myconius recover completely, but he lived two months after Luther's death.

If God planned you before the world began, do you think He would make it hard for you to find His will? Some people think that the will of God is like an invisible door which you've got to find. And God is standing behind it, and when you walk past it God says, "Ha, ha, you missed. Too bad for you."

Ruth was gleaning and Boaz just happened to see her. From that "chance" meeting, she became the great-grandmother of David, and ultimately an ancestor of Jesus Himself.

Wisdom & Understanding

A man said to a pastor that he'd give him $10,000 if he'd say his brother Jim was an angel at his funeral. The pastor agreed. He got up to do the eulogy. "Jim was the most dishonest man in town. He was foul-mouthed, a drunkard, and a lying, cheating gambler. Nobody trusted him. He was always getting into fights, beat his wife and kids, and never did anything nice for his family." The man was getting ready to jump up and shoot the preacher when he said, "But compared to his brother Fred, he was an angel."

Albert Einstein remarked in 1932 that "there is not the slightest indication that nuclear energy will ever be obtainable." Thomas Edison thought alternating current would be a waste of time. Franklin Delano Roosevelt once predicted, when he was Assistant Secretary of the U.S. Navy, that airplanes would never be useful in battle against a fleet of ships. There's nothing like the passage of time to make the world's smartest people look like complete idiots. So let's look at a few more. In 1883 Lord Kelvin, president of the Royal Society and no mean scientist himself, predicted that "X rays will prove to be a hoax." When Gary Cooper turned down the Rhett Butler role in *Gone With The Wind*, he is said to have remarked, "I'm just glad it will be Clark Gable who's falling flat on his face and not Gary Cooper." "Everything that can be invented, has been invented," announced Charles H. Duell, commissioner of the U.S. Patents Office – in 1899.[147]

A Boston man was entertaining a famous Chinese scholar. Barely giving his friend time to breathe, he rushed him to the subway saying, "If we can just catch this next train, we'll save ourselves three minutes." The scholar looked at him and asked, "And what significant thing will we do with the three minutes we are saving?"

Witness

A young girl is walking home from church on Sunday and says to her mother, "Mummy, didn't you tell me that God was so big that the world can't contain Him,

---

[147] *Time Magazine* 25-10-04 p 47

that the earth is like His footstool, and that you can't see the end of Him." "That's right," said her mother. "Well, today we learned that God lives inside of me." "That's right too honey." "I'm confused. If God is so big that He can't even fit in the world, and He also lives inside of me, shouldn't people see Him coming out of me?"

Salt is no good in a salt shaker.

Salt is a minority in anything it occupies.

I'd rather see a sermon
Than hear one any day;
I'd rather one should walk with me
Than merely tell the way.
The eye's a better pupil,
More willing than the ear;
Fine counsel is confusing,
But example's always clear.
And the best of all the preachers
Are the men who live their creeds;
For to see good put in action
Is what everybody needs. Edgar A. Guest.

Joe the derelict was saved, delivered from alcoholism, and so thankful that he'd do anything for the Lord, even menial tasks like cleaning, washing dishes, and mowing the lawn. Then he met another derelict, took him home, cleaned him up, cleaned his vomit, and nursed him through the bad times. "I just want to be like Joe," said the derelict to a church worker. "You mean you want to be like Jesus." replied the worker. "Is He like Joe?" asked the derelict.

A man gave his life to the Lord and told his business partner. His partner was overjoyed and said, "That's fantastic. I'm a Christian too." The new Christian looked at him and said, "I didn't know that. You're actually the main reason I didn't become a Christian years ago. I thought that since you were such a good person without being a Christian, there was no reason for me to be one either."

I might have entered the ministry if certain clergymen I knew had not looked and acted so much like undertakers. Oliver Wendell Holmes

Robert Louis Stevenson wrote in his diary, "I have been to church today, and am not depressed."

Live in such a way that you would not be ashamed to sell your parrot to the town gossip. Will Rogers

A stressed out woman was tailgating a man as they drove along. As he slowed to stop at an amber light, she gestured angrily, swore and screamed, and blasted her horn. While she was thus engaged, she heard a tap on the window where a policeman stood. He ordered her out of the car and she was promptly arrested, taken to the police station, and put in a holding cell. Sometime later, the policeman returned saying, "I'm sorry, Ma'am. When I pulled up behind you, I noticed your 'What Would Jesus Do?' and 'Follow Me To Church' bumper stickers, saw the way you behaved, and I figured your car must have been stolen."

Witty Sayings

The roundest knight at King Arthur's round table was Sir Cumference. He acquired his size from too much pi.

A hole was found in a nudist camp wall. The police are looking into it.

I wondered why the baseball kept getting bigger. Then it hit me.

Sign on the lawn at a drug rehab centre: Keep Off The Grass.

Women

One day, spotting a lamp by the roadside, a man picked it up, rubbed it furiously, and a genie appeared. "I'll grant you one wish," said the genie. The man thought for a while, then said, "I want an amazing job. I want a job that no man has ever succeeded at or even attempted to do." "Well," said the genie. "There's only one job for you." And he turned him into a housewife."

The reason the average woman would rather have beauty than brains is she knows the average man can see better than he can think. James Dobson

23% of men want sex every day, compared to only 8% of women.[148] (Now there's a recipe for disaster!)

Wanted ad for the most difficult job in the world: Must be competent in accounting, art, community relations, cuisine, decorating, designing, economics, education, energy, entertainment, fashion, geriatrics, handicraft, horticulture, law, literature, management, maintenance, mediation, medicine, paediatrics, psychology, purchasing, recreation, religion, romance, transportation. The job? Housewife!

Three men were out fishing when one caught a mermaid. "I'll give you each a wish if you let me go," she said. "Double my intelligence," said the first man. Immediately, he began reciting Shakespeare. "Wow!" said the second man. "Triple my intelligence." Immediately, he began expounding Einstein's Theory of Relativity. "Wow!" said the third man. "Quadruple my intelligence." "Are you sure? You may not like the

---

[148] *Reader's Digest* April 2005 p 18

results." "I'm sure." Immediately, he turned into a woman.

Question: How many women with PMS does it take to change a light bulb? Answer: One! *Just one!* Do you know *why* it takes just one? Because there's nobody else in the house who knows *how* to change a light bulb! In fact, they'd be lucky even to notice that the bulb had *blown!* They'd probably sit around *in the dark* for three days before they even noticed, and then they wouldn't be able to find the bulb that's been sitting in the *same cupboard* for the last *three years!*

Women don't want to hear what you think. Women want to hear what they think – in a deeper voice. Bill Cosby

One woman complained that her clothes were so old that they were all made in Australia.

Words

Keep your words soft and sweet; one day, you may have to eat them.

Even the merest hint of praise or scorn can affect our performance. A recent study, published in the journal *Perceptual and Motor Skills*, demonstrated how powerful a few words can be. Forty competitive tennis players were shown digital images of balls coming their way. Just before each ball appeared, the players saw or heard comments like "good shot" or "bad shot". The reaction times of players hearing negative remarks were measurably slower.[149]

Work

It's true hard work never killed anyone, but I figure, why take the chance? Ronald Reagan

---

[149] *Reader's Digest* June 2006 p 127

Many employers motivate their employees with bonuses. Others offer gyms and a few even provide day care. Our company has gone a step further with a sign that reads: "Employee Incentive Plan. Work or Get Fired!" Susan Rhea

A man went to his doctor and asked for a certificate for time off work. His doctor said, "You're just plain lazy." "Give me a medical name, because I have to report back to my wife."

Opportunity is missed by most people because it is dressed in overalls and looks like work. Thomas Edison

Hard work pays off in the future; laziness pays off now.

The great composer does not set to work because he is inspired, but becomes inspired because he is working. Bach, Beethoven, Wagner and Mozart settled down day after day to the job with as much regularity as an accountant settles down each day in his figures. They didn't waste time waiting for inspiration. Ernest Newman.

Unusual jobs: More than 8700 workers have listed the most unconventional jobs they've ever held in a survey on careerbuilder.com. Top picks are: autopsy assistant, bartender at the Liberace mansion, cat nanny, donkey trainer, elf at Santa's workshop, FBI fingerprint examiner, grave digger, hurricane hunter, ice sculpture carver, junk mail machine operator, kitty litter box decorator, laser tag referee, magician's assistant, nuclear electrician on a submarine, opera singer, parachute tester, quality control taster for a chocolate factory, romance specialist, scratcher (scratching backs of patients), turkey wrangler, undercover vice decoy, video game tester, wallpaper peeler, x-ray technician for zoo animals, yawn counter at a sleep clinic, Zamboni (ice resurfacer) driver.[150]

Worldliness

The church that marries the spirit of the age will be a widow in the next.

"World" in the New Testament usage is a sociological order established by man which rejects the righteous government of God over man and in particular rejects God's righteous governor the Lord Jesus Christ. So the world is a congregation of rebels. Derek Prince

Examples of conformity are everywhere. One time, as I looked into a fir tree, a part of it moved. As I looked more closely, I realised that it was a stick insect blending into its surroundings. If people can't tell the difference between you and the rest of your peers, you have blended in, you have conformed to the world.

Worship

A man can no more diminish God's glory by refusing to worship Him than a lunatic can put out the sun by scribbling the word "darkness" on the walls of his cell. C.S. Lewis in *The Problem Of Pain*

Writing

1. Avoid alliteration. Always. 2. Prepositions are not words to end sentences with. 3. Avoid clichés like the plague. (They're old hat.) 4. Employ the vernacular. 5. Eschew ampersands & abbreviations, etc. 6. Parenthetical remarks (however relevant) are unnecessary. 7. It is wrong to ever split an infinitive. 8. Contractions aren't necessary. 9. Foreign words and phrases are not *apropos*. 10. One should never

---

[150] *Reader's Digest* December, 2008, p 18

generalise. 11. Eliminate quotations. As Ralph Waldo Emerson once said: "I hate quotations. Tell me what you know." 12. Comparisons are as bad as clichés. 13. Don't be redundant; don't use more words than necessary; it's highly superfluous. 14. Be more or less specific. 15. Understatement is always best. 16. Exaggeration is a billion times worse than understatement. 17. One-word sentences? Eliminate. 18. Analogies in writing are like feathers on a snake. 19. The passive voice is to be avoided. 20. Go around the barn at high noon to avoid colloquialisms. 21. Even if a mixed metaphor sings, it should be derailed. 22. Who needs rhetorical questions? Source unknown

George Simenon was a Belgian mystery writer who wrote over 200 novels. He created Inspector Maigret... Faster than Maigret could solve his cases, Simenon wrote them. At the rate of 80 typewritten pages a day, he could finish a book in 8 to 10 days.[151]

Yielding

Trying to maintain control in your life as a Christian is like holding one side of a horse's reins while the Lord holds the other side. It's going to cause major problems.

A man had a 2-storey house. He heard a knocking, opened the door, and found Jesus there, so he invited Him to live in the house and gave Him a room in the top floor. Jesus will only take what you give Him. That night, the man was sleeping and heard a pounding on the door, opened the door a crack and the devil barged in. He had a terrible fight, trying to resist the devil and his temptations, yelling out for

---

[151] Ballinger, Erich *Detective Dictionary: A Handbook for Aspiring Sleuths* p110, translated by Catherine Kerkhoff

help all the time. Eventually, he managed to throw the devil out. In the morning, he said to the Lord, "Why didn't You help me last night? Couldn't You hear me calling for help?" Jesus said, "The problem is, you've got this whole big house to yourself, and I've only got one room." The man replied, "Ah, I see your point. You can have the whole top floor, and I'll keep the bottom floor." The man was sleeping that night and heard a pounding on the door, opened the door a crack and the devil barged in again. He had another terrible fight, trying to resist the devil and his temptations, yelling out for help all the time. Eventually, he managed to throw the devil out. In the morning, he said, "Why didn't You help me last night? Couldn't You hear me calling for help?" Jesus said, "The problem is, I have the top floor, but you still have the bottom floor to yourself." The man answered, "Ah, I see what you mean. From now on, the whole house is yours." That night, the man was asleep, and there was a pounding at the door again. This time, Jesus went to the door, opened it wide, and stood in the doorway. The devil looked at Him, bowed very low, and said, "I'm sorry, but I think I knocked on the wrong door."[152]

To feed the 5,000, you don't have to go to the shop to buy food. You need to find the little boy who doesn't have much, but is willing to submit it to the Lord.

Youth

When I look at today's young people I fear for the future of civilisation. Aristotle (Born 384 BC)

Alfred Tennyson wrote his first volume at 18. Napoleon had conquered Italy at 27. Byron and

---

[152] I originally heard this parable told by Reinhard Bonnke.

Raphael both died at 37. Isaac Newton devised the Law of Gravity at 24. Victor Hugo wrote a tragedy at 15. Poet John Keats lived a mere 26 years. Franz Schubert died at 31 having written more than 110 musical compositions. Bell patented the telephone at 29. James Watt started work on the steam engine at 24, the same age that Charles Dickens wrote *Pickwick Papers*. Edison at 26 was already famous. Westinghouse invented air brakes at 22. Einstein propounded the theory of relativity at 26. Pasteur revolutionised chemistry at 25.

Zeal

Nobody likes to see an old barn, but everyone loves to see an old barn burn. Vince Esterman

It is easier to cool down a fanatic than to warm up a corpse. Trevor Chandler

Made in the USA
Middletown, DE
17 May 2021